A TRILOGY OF CONSECRATION:

The Courier, The Historian and The Missionary

Boris Handal

Published: July 2020
Boris Handal

A Trilogy of Consecration: The Courier, the Historian and the Missionary
Print: 978-0-6489014-3-3
e-book: 978-0-6489014-4-0

Table of Contents

Introduction i

Table of Illustrations v

Acknowledgements vii

SHAYKH SALMÁN 3

1. The Courier of God 3

1.1 A Great Emissary 4
1.2 Arrested in Istanbul 7
1.3 Detained in Syria 8
1.4 Delivering the Tablets 10

2. "The Bábí-Maker" 12

2.1 Saved by the Providence 13
2.2 A Person of Fine Judgment 15
2.3 The Story of Muḥammad-Báqir-i-Qazvíní 16
2.4 The Wedding of 'Abdu'l-Bahá 18

3. The Pen of the Blessed Beauty Addresses Salmán 21

3.1 Tablet of Salmán I (Revealed in Baghdád) 22
3.2 Tablet of Salmán II (Revealed in Adrianople) 23
3.3 Tablet of Salmán III (Revealed in 'Akká) 25

4. An Explanation of the Tablet to Salmán Revealed in Adrianople - by Adib Taherzadeh 25

YÁR-MUḤAMMAD-I-ZARANDÍ 36

1. Nabíl the Scholar 38

1.1 The Chronicler 38
1.2 A Laureate Poet 40

2. His indefatigable disciple 48

2.1 The Initial Contact 48
2.2 In Ṭihrán 50
2.3 In 'Iráq, Kirmánsháh and Baghdád 54
2.4 After the Martyrdom of the Báb 58
2.5 "Oh for the joy of those days ..." 61
2.6 Missions in Constantinople and Adrianople 65

2.7 An Important Mission in Egypt 70
2.8 In the Holy Land 78

3. Tablets to Nabíl 88

MULLÁ ṢÁDIQ 97

1. Paving the Way 98
2. Accepting the New Faith 101
3. An Excellent Global Proclamation 106
4. Spreading the Seeds of Faith 108
5. Among the Companions of Tabarsí 110
6. In Baghdád 113
7. In the Síyáh Chal 115
8. Pilgrimage to 'Akká 118

Bibliography 124

Introduction

The upcoming centenary of the Ascension of 'Abdu'l-Bahá is an occasion for the celebration of His life and those of His closest devotees. 'Abdu'l-Bahá always took pride in the believers' achievements and was very generous in praising their qualities and spirit of service. In His talks and writings, 'Abdu'l-Bahá referred from time to time to their sacrifices and how their detachment assisted in the growth of the Cause of Bahá'u'lláh.

During 1915 'Abdu'l-Bahá gave a series of talks to the Haifa Bahá'í community highlighting sixty-nine believers whom He particularly admired for their services to the Faith of God. 'Abdu'l-Bahá Himself was present at many of the events related in the stories He told. These talks were printed as a book in 1924, with Shoghi Effendi's permission, under the title *Memorials of the Faithful*.[1, 2]

This book depicts the lives of three of these sixty-nine believers who associated with 'Abdu'l-Bahá at different stages of His life throughout the Heroic Age of the Bahá'í Faith. The Heroic Age began with the Báb's Declaration of His Mission in 1844, continued throughout the ministry of Bahá'u'lláh, and culminated with 'Abdu'l-Bahá's Ascension in 1921. The culmination of the Heroic Age marked, simultaneously, the beginning of the first century of the Formative Age, whose auspicious first centenary will be celebrated in 2021.

In this trilogy the lives of Shaykh Salmán, Nabíl-i-A'zam and Mullá Ṣádiq are narrated, as well as important events associated with their lives. They came from diverse social backgrounds, but had consecration to the Lord of the Age in common. Shaykh Salmán was the on-foot courier between two remote countries. Nabíl-i-A'zam was

---

[1] Moojan Momen. Memorials of the Faithful: The Democratization of Sainthood. *Lights of Irfan*, vol. 17, 2015, pp. 205-224. Available online at: http://irfancolloquia.org/pdf/lights17_momen_sainthood.pdf

[2] 'Abdu'l-Bahá. *Memorials of the Faithful*. Wilmette, Bahá'í Publishing Trust, 1971, p. 5.

the chronicler that carefully documented events which otherwise would have been obliterated by the passing of time. Mullá Ṣádiq stood out as the one who travelled broadly converting people to the new Faith with wisdom, dignity and grace. The first was illiterate, while the second was a self-made scholar who started out in life as a shepherd, whereas Mullá Ṣádiq came from an educated family of means.

They were all exposed to the magical experience of reaching the presence of Bahá'u'lláh at various times and for extensive periods. Only one of them, Mullá Ṣádiq the oldest of the three men, had the additional privilege of meeting the Báb. Each of them treasured forever the singular experience of meeting a Divine Messenger, an opportunity that has been likened to attaining the presence of God Himself.[3]

Empowered by such inestimable blessings, they abandoned all other concerns and adapted their personal lives to meeting the needs of the Cause. They dedicated themselves completely to service as the ultimate manifestation of love for their Lord. Nabíl-i-A'zam and Shaykh Salmán survived the Ascension of Bahá'u'lláh in 1892. The former for only a few days, and the latter for seven years. They remained firm in the Covenant, ever loyal and obedient to 'Abdu'l-Bahá.

The Revelation of Bahá'u'lláh transformed them into spiritual giants and made of them champions in the arena of dedication and detachment. To their wonder, amazing capacities and invincible powers became theirs, which made it possible for them to endure the most formidable vicissitudes with an ever-increasing spirit of faith and certitude. After glimpsing the greatness of such a Message and the lights of paradise, nothing had the power to deter them in the path of service — not age, nor lack of means, nor family circumstances, nor the constant danger of being beaten and killed.

Although no one assigned them the roles of courier, historian or missionary, each found his identity walking a path of service, and each discovered his inner attributes while on his personal journey. Empowered by faith, certitude, and love of Bahá'u'lláh these three

[3]The Báb. Selections from the Writings of the Báb. US Bahá'í Publishing Trust, 1982, p. 77.

men became a new creation, the like of whom we rarely see in human existence. Shaykh Salmán became the "Messenger of the Merciful"[4] and His "Bábí-Maker"[5], Nabíl-i-A'zam became "His Poet-Laureate, His chronicler and His indefatigable disciple" [6] whereas Mullá Ṣádiq was designated "The Name of God, the Most Truthful"[7].

Writing of his service to the Cause of God, 'Abdu'l-Bahá said of Shaykh Salmán that he became "the means for its spread, and contributing to the happiness of the believers"[8]. In turn, Nabíl-i-A'zam was referred to as a "torch in every company ... the star of every assemblage"[9] and Mullá Ṣádiq was called a "surging sea, a falcon that soared high".[10]

Like incandescent lamps, warmth and light shone generously from them to others. Thus they were able to attract hearts and minds to the same Source that was giving them energy. Like an ever-advancing and consuming fire devouring any trivial matter in its path, triumphing over any fear, with courage and bravery, these illustrious servants pressed forward with the certitude that their Lord was with them at all times.

Reading the three stories that follow may prompt an inclination to reflect on profound existential questions: What is the spiritual reality shown to these men that spurred them to such heights of servitude? What is it like to be sustained by such superior forces? How can we access that reality and those forces and thus walk our own path of service with such love, excellence and free of all attachment to reward?

---

[4]Adib Taherzadeh. The *Revelation of Bahá'u'lláh*, vol 3. George Ronald Oxford, 1974, p. 175

[5]Youness Afroukhteh. *Memories of Nine Years in 'Akká* (translated by Riaz Masrour). George Ronald Oxford, 2004, p.228

[6]Shoghi Effendi. *God Passes By.* US Bahá'í Publishing Trust, 1979, p. 130.

[7]'Abdu'l-Bahá. *Memorials of the Faithful.* Wilmette, Bahá'í Publishing Trust, 1971, p. 5.

[8]'Abdu'l-Bahá. *Memorials of the Faithful.* Wilmette, Bahá'í Publishing Trust, 1971, p. 15.

[9]'Abdu'l-Bahá. Memorials of the Faithful. Wilmette, Bahá'í Publishing Trust, 1971, p. 34.

[10]'Abdu'l-Bahá. *Memorials of the Faithful.* Wilmette, Bahá'í Publishing Trust, 1971, p. 8.

How can we acquire detachment and fulfil our spiritual destiny? What are our own God-given gifts that require effort and volition to be manifest? What is missing from our thoughts, words, choices and habits that leads us to continue to fall short of this exalted station? Our questions might be similar to the words of a poem by Nabíl who admonishes himself thus:[11]

> O Nabíl, make a plan for thine own affairs; thou art forty years old; make a change; ask for the cup of spiritual knowledge from God this year; how long wilt thou stick in the world of Words?
>
> Thine age is forty, yet thou art nought but a fool; thou hast not entered in at the gate of the City of the Heart: they say that forty is the year of perfection: "thine age is forty, yet hast thou not become perfect."

At the commemoration of 'Abdu'l-Bahá's Ascension may we remember the utter consecration of believers like Salmán, Nabíl-i-A'zam and Mullá Ṣádiq who, by their constant striving for perfection and tireless sacrifice in the path of giving the best of themselves to their Lord, became saints and heroes.

Boris Handal
Sydney, Australia

[11]Adapted from Edward Granville Browne. The Bábís of Persia II – Their Literature and Doctrines. *The Journal of the Royal Asiatic Society of Great Britain and Ireland,* vol. 4, No. 4, 1889, pp. 881-1009.

Table of Illustrations

Figure 1: Shaykh Salmán. Courtesy: Bahá'í Media 37

Figure 2: The land gate of 'Akká from inside the city.
Courtesy: Bahá'í Media 38

Figure 3: The barracks in 'Akka were Bahá'u'lláh was imprisoned.
Courtesy: Bahá'í Media 39

Figure 4: Bahá'u'lláh's cell in the Prison of 'Akká.
Courtesy: Bahá'í Media 39

Figure 5: Map of Irán. Courtesy: Pedro Donaires 40

Figure 6: Nabíl-i-A'ẓam..40

Figure 7: Bahá'ís in Adrianople. Courtesy: Bahá'í Media...........41

Figure 8: A street in 'Akká c. 1914. Courtesy: Bahá'í Media 99

Figure 9: The House of 'Abbúd in 'Akká where Bahá'u'lláh resided.
Courtesy: Bahá'í Media 100

Figure 10: Cities associated with Bahá'í history.
Courtesy: Pedro Donaires 100

Figure 11: Ibn-i-Aṣdaq, son of Mullá Ṣádiq.........................101

Figure 12: A view of Baghdad in the nineteenth century.
Courtesy: Bahá'í Media.................................101

Figure 13: Original corridor to the entrance of the Síyáh-Chál in
Tehran...102

Figure 14: Aerial view of city of 'Akká, May 1972.
Courtesy: Bahá'í Media.................................102

Acknowledgements

I would like to acknowledge the editorial assistance rendered by Nur Mihrshahi and Melanie Lotfali as well as to Pedro Donaires for the maps and Fariba Heydari Rosas for the cover concept design. I also would like to thank my wife Parvin for her support and patience while I researched and wrote this book.

<u>SH</u>AY<u>KH</u> SALMÁN

"THE MESSENGER OF THE MERCIFUL"

A humble man without learning, but filled with the Holy Spirit, is more powerful than the most nobly-born profound scholar without that inspiration.

'Abdu'l-Bahá[1]

[1]'Abdu'l-Bahá. *Paris Talks.* UK Bahá'í Publishing Trust, 1972, p. 165.

Shaykh Salmán

1. The Courier of God

Shaykh Salmán is known in Bahá'í history as the "Messenger of the Merciful" (Payk-i-Raḥmán), [1] the one who for many years acted as a courier between the believers in Iran and Bahá'u'lláh in the Holy Land. This chapter examines the nature of his services and recounts stories associated with his continuous and arduous travels. A discussion of the content of the Tablets of Bahá'u'lláh revealed in Shaykh Salmán's honour is presented at the end.

Shaykh Salmán was the name that Bahá'u'lláh conferred upon Shaykh Khanjan [2], one of His most beloved disciples. In doing that, the Blessed Beauty was evoking the memory of his namesake Salmán, the faithful messenger of Prophet Muḥammad whose original name was *Ruzbeh.*

Shaykh Salmán came from a very poor family. He never attended school and therefore, his acquired knowledge was limited, and he was illiterate. However, his school was life itself and his mentors were Bahá'u'lláh and 'Abdu'l-Bahá Who showed him much affection.

This faithful and dedicated Bahá'í heard for the first time about the Faith of the Báb sometime between the end of 1849 and the beginning of the year 1850. He embraced the Cause of God in his native village of Hindíyán, southwest of Iran, on the shores of the Persian Gulf. Immediately after his declaration of faith, he travelled on foot to the city of Tehran, 1000 km away, in order to meet the congregation of Bábís [3] in the capital.

By listening to the talks and conversations of the friends of God, Shaykh Salmán gradually became familiar with the teachings of the Faith, to the extent that he understood and could address profound

---

[1]Adib Taherzadeh. *The Revelation of Bahá'u'lláh*, vol 3. George Ronald Oxford, 1974, p. 175

[2]Interestingly, the word Khanjan means "dagger" in Farsi.

[3]Bábís were followers of the Faith of the Báb.

questions with ease, despite his lack of formal education. According to a believer who met him:

> To visit this great soul is a joy beyond measure for any of the believers. Though he was illiterate and his manner of life was extremely simple, he was the essence of intelligence and knowledge. Whenever the friends became entangled in some difficult question, he was able to answer the question and explain the matter under discussion in a few simple words. We never witnessed in him the slightest trace of self, which creeps so insidiously into the hearts of men. [4]

Like so many simple souls who appeared at the beginning of the apostolic days of each Manifestation of God, he shone by his candour, his simplicity and his intuitive understanding. Saint Peter, who was also illiterate, serves as a parallel from Christendom.

Shaykh Salmán was certainly the embodiment of Shoghi Effendi's words:

> How often—and the early history of the Faith in the land of its birth offers many a striking testimony—have the lowliest adherents of the Faith, unschooled and utterly inexperienced, and with no standing whatever, and in some cases devoid of intelligence, been capable of winning victories for their Cause, before which the most brilliant achievements of the learned, the wise, and the experienced have paled. [5]

1.1 A Great Emissary

In the year 1853, when Bahá'u'lláh was banished to 'Iráq by order of the Iranian government, Shaykh Salmán was the first to arrive in His presence and receive His ceaseless blessings.

On that occasion, Bahá'u'lláh revealed Tablets to the believers of Hindíyán and it was Shaykh Salmán who on his return was commissioned to deliver them to Iran. Thus began the lifelong services of Shaykh Salmán as the messenger of the Manifestation of God.

---

[4]Hájí Mírzá Haydar 'Alí. *Stories from the Delight of Hearts - Memoirs of Hájí Mírzá Haydar 'Alí.* (translated by Abu'l-Qasim Faizí). Kalimat Press, 1995. p. 133.

[5]Shoghi Effendi. *The Advent of Divine Justice.* US Bahá'í Publishing Trust, 1990, p. 45.

The love of the Blessed Beauty transformed him and made him shine forth with the spirit of sacrifice and loyalty, perhaps the most valuable attributes of Shaykh Salmán. He could not, like other distinguished believers, transcribe the Sacred Words, or speak eloquently to a congregation at a mosque or hold a scholarly conversation with a learned theologian, nor appear with poise in front of the aristocracy or in government circles. What he could do however, was to place himself under Bahá'u'lláh's direction and try, as faithfully as possible, to serve Him with devotion. And thus Shaykh Salmán rendered his memorable services for many years and amid so much adversity.

Though the year of his birth is unknown, it is known that for over forty years Shaykh Salmán was in charge of distributing the Tablets that Bahá'u'lláh revealed, from Baghdád, Turkey and the prison-city of 'Akká to the believers in Iran. He also brought written supplications from the Persian friends to the various places of exile. Such a service was extended after Bahá'u'lláh's Ascension and into 'Abdu'l-Bahá's ministry. his devoted courier work for the Cause of God, Bahá'u'lláh called him the "Messenger of the Merciful."[6]

The important role played by Shaykh Salmán also extended to other roles such as brightening the hearts of the believers in the Cradle of the Faith by bringing to them recent news of their Beloved from His exile. Every year he would make one of those trips.

As Bahá'u'lláh's emissary, throughout all those years, he visited dispersed Bahá'í communities throughout Iran travelling along dangerous roads notorious for the presence of thieves and robbers. There was also the constant risk of being discovered and arrested by Muslim fanatics. Usually on foot, the arduous journeys sometimes took up to six months, as Shaykh Salmán travelled all the way from Iran to the Holy Land. He carried scores of letters in the form of requests from the believers or responses from Bahá'u'lláh. Despite the challenges, Shaykh Salmán was able to carry out his missions with efficiency, courage, reliability and great physical strength. It has been said that on those extensive trips his diet consisted primarily of bread and onions.

[6]Adib Taherzadeh. *The Revelation of Bahá'u'lláh*, vol 3. George Ronald Oxford, 1974, p. 175

Shaykh Salmán was one of the first to arrive at the prison-city of 'Akká when Bahá'u'lláh was exiled there in August 1868. [7] It was very dangerous to smuggle the sacred Tablets out of the prison-city of 'Akká and into the Iranian cities. In those times the cities were walled and outsiders were checked at the entrance gates for several purposes including customs.

Despite the setbacks, in all those years of exemplary work Shaykh Salmán never failed. None of those precious letters were ever lost or stolen. However, he was a frequent victim of persecution like any other Bábí and Bahá'í. More than once, he had to endure the tortures and punishments that the hands of the fanatics inflicted upon him. Nevertheless, his faith never faltered nor did his constancy dwindle. "Over and over again, in Iṣfahán," said 'Abdu'l-Bahá, "he was subjected to severe trials, but he remained patient and thankful under all conditions..." [8]

Sometimes he was arrested on suspicion and asked to disclose the believers' names — a request that he flatly refused. Nor did he allow the sacred Tablets to fall into the hands of the clergy and authorities.

In brief, due to the excellence of his Bahá'í work for over four decades, his acute spiritual judgment, his devotion to the Blessed Beauty and the qualities of his soul he managed to achieve great victories for the Cause of God.

When Bahá'u'lláh's Ascension took place in 1892, Shaykh Salmán, already advanced in years, was very sad. But unlike others at the time, he remained firm in obedience to 'Abdu'l-Bahá, the designated Center of the Covenant of Bahá'u'lláh. He continued to serve his Master with the same simple heart, going to and coming from the Holy Land, until when he died in the city of Shíráz in 1899.

'Abdu'l-Bahá from time to time recounted the inspiring story of Shayhk Salmán to the believers. For example, thirteen years later after his passing 'Abdu'l-Bahá telling the American Bahá'ís about such a beautiful soul. According to His chronicler: "That evening 'Abdu'l-

[7] Moojan Momen. *Bahá'u'lláh: A Short Biography.* London, Oneworld Publications, 2007.

[8] 'Abdu'l-Bahá. *Memorials of the Faithful.* Wilmette, Bahá'í Publishing Trust, 1971, p.15.

Bahá spoke of the days of the Blessed Beauty and of His kindness towards Shaykh Salmán. He praised the sincerity and constancy of that messenger of the Merciful and described some of the events in his life".[9]

1.2 Arrested in Istanbul

At the instigation of the Iranian ambassador, Shaykh Salmán was arrested on one occasion while in the city of Istanbul, capital of the Ottoman Empire. At the time he was on his way to 'Akká carrying many letters from the believers to Bahá'u'lláh. He had hidden the correspondence in a special lining inside his long coat to avoid it being discovered. Shaykh Salmán recounts:

> When I arrived at the city's gate, one of the officials stopped me and I inquired as to why I was being seized. "The [Iranian] Ambassador has asked for you," he responded. When we arrived at the embassy, the Ambassador said, "Since the eventide has advanced, for now put him and his haversack in an empty room until tomorrow morning."
>
> After I entered the room, I said to them, "I am an old man and frequently will get thirsty. Kindly bring me a parch of water." They brought the water. I was bewildered what to do with the missives I carried [for Bahá'u'lláh]. If I burned them, what would I do with the ashes? If I tore them, where would I hide the shreds? Suddenly it occurred to me that the best course of action was to shred them into small pieces and to swallow them with the aid of water. I proceeded to do so. I remember that I was very upset over swallowing one of the letters that had been penned on a very thick paper. When morrow came, my bag was inspected and no traces of letters were found and, therefore, they had to release me.
>
> When I had attained the presence of Bahá'u'lláh, I said to Him, "O Blessed Beauty! I ate all the missives. Now it's up to You to answer the friends!"

---

[9]Mahmud Zarqani. *Mahmud's Diary: The Diary of Mirza Mahmud-I-Zarqani: Chronicling 'Abdu'l Baha's Journey to America* (translated by Mohi Sobhani). George Ronald Oxford, 1998, p.182.

From that date, <u>Sh</u>ay<u>kh</u> Salmán never travelled by the way of Istanbul. [10]

1.3 Detained in Syria

On another occasion, around the year of 1870, <u>Sh</u>ay<u>kh</u> Salmán was coming from Iran enroute to 'Akká. When passing through the city of Aleppo in Syria he was arrested carrying about three hundred prayers of the Bahá'ís. Immediately they confiscated everything he had and the Mu<u>sh</u>íru'd-Dawlih, the Iranian Ambassador who was passing through that city put him under investigation. <u>Sh</u>ay<u>kh</u> Salmán himself related the details of what happened at that time:

> On an evening, he [Mu<u>sh</u>íru'd-Dawlih,] and the consuls with their entourage were pacing up and down the courtyard. I saw him and heard him say:
>
> 'We believed and were certain that the Cause of Bahá'u'lláh was a political cause, and that His aim was to obtain power and sovereignty and amass riches to make a name for Himself. Therefore we tried hard to put Him down and made plans accordingly. No matter how much we harmed Him, no matter how many times we banished Him - and we contended with Him backed by the full powers of two states - indeed, no matter what we did, His power and authority and fame, His greatness and grandeur were enhanced. We were much amazed, lost in wonderment trying to find the reason. Now I see that this man [Salmán] has something like three hundred petitions with him. In these, there is no mention at all of politics, government, state and nation. Notwithstanding all the injuries, notwithstanding imprisonments, banishments, executions, and pillages inflicted on the Bahá'ís all this time, no mention is made of them and there is no complaint. These petitions he carries all consist of supplications, and are confined entirely to spiritual matters such as:
>
> "O God! Keep me safe from the evil of selfish and carnal desires, give me constancy, make me steadfast in Thy love,

---

[10] Mírzá Habíbu'lláh Afnán. *Memories of the Báb, Bahá'u'lláh and 'Abdu'l-Bahá* (Translated and Annotated by Ahang Rabbani). An electronic-publication of Kalimat Press, 2005, pp. 206-207.

bestow on me the bounty of servitude, confirm me in service to Thy Cause, make me free of all else save Thee, confirm us that we may serve the people of all the world, kiss the hand of the executioner and hands clapping, feet dancing, hurry to the scaffold."'

Then he called for two or three of those petitions and had them read aloud. They all admired the eloquence and the excellence of style and composition. Then he [Mushíru'd-Dawlih,] said:

> Why should we repress such people who love God, seek God and speak of God? In His Book, the Qur'án, God has related the story of the believer in the household of Pharaoh, so as to warn us, remind us, and make us remember that should there be falsehood, the one who is false will not endure, but if the one whom we are contending with is the bearer of truth, it will all rebound upon us and will finish us; we shall be the losers and pay a heavy penalty. Nothing detrimental to the nation and to the state has been witnessed in their deeds, or reflected in their words. Whatever has been heard has come either from their enemies, from those who deny them, or from those bereft of knowledge. Moreover, we have all seen, and it has been our experience, that the more we tried to repress them, the more we insulted and denigrated them, the more we encompassed their death and extermination, the greater became their number, and the more their strength and power, their might and fame. Now they are living in the utmost of health, of glory, of bliss.'

Mushíru'd-Dawlih, was speaking in this manner, and others were saying that they agreed with him, quoting instances. The next morning he sent for me, apologized to me, and said:

> 'We had been misled. I am very grateful to you, because you have made me see the truth of the matter. Government ought not to interfere in spiritual affairs, in matters connected with faith and conscience.'
>
> He restored to me all the petitions, and told his men to bring all the merchandise and other articles which had been

> confiscated, and in his own presence they were given back to me. And he wrote a letter of recommendation to the vice-consul in Beirut, telling him:
>
> 'Give the Shaykh the utmost consideration and protection, and see that he reaches 'Akká with all that he has with him, to the presence of Haḍrat-i-'Abbás Effendi ['Abdu'l-Bahá].'

Then he said to me:

> 'Kiss His hands on my behalf, offer Him my apologies, ask for His forgiveness, and beg for confirmation that I may be enabled to make redress for the past.' [11]

It was therefore through Shaykh Salmán, that this senior official of the Iranian government became friendly and sympathetic to Bahá'u'lláh, and henceforth always tried to protect the Bahá'ís and praised their teachings. Although years before he had been responsible for the exiles of Bahá'u'lláh to Constantinople (Istanbul), Adrianople and 'Akká, he came to manifest the utmost respect for the Faith.

1.4 Delivering the Tablets

Shaykh Salmán was an unassuming man with a modest appearance. The following story portrays how simple was this man and yet how special was his spiritual wisdom:

> Before our arrival in Shíráz, in the village of Zarqán, Shaykh Salmán sent a letter to Hájí Siyyid Ismá'íl-i-Azghandí [a Bahá'í] requesting him to come and meet us outside the city. The reason for this was that Shaykh Salmán had a number of Tablets and other Bahá'í relics with him and as a precaution he wanted this man to take them to Shíráz, because each passenger travelling with the caravan would be searched by officials before entering the city.
>
> In response to this letter, Hájí Siyyid Ismá'íl came on his donkey to Zarqán and took the Tablets and other articles with him to Shíráz. We ourselves followed him in due course and after being searched at the check-point went straight

[11] Hasan Balyuzi. *Bahá'u'lláh, the King of Glory.* George Ronald Oxford, 1991, pp. 441-443.

to his house in Shíráz. Our host used to spend much of his time in the company of Mushíru'l-Mulk. [12] The latter had recently retired from his government post and his nephew had succeeded him in this high office. Since his retirement Mushíru'l-Mulk used to spend most of his time in his country home. It was through his gardener there..., a Bahá'í, that he was attracted to the Faith.

Soon after his conversion, Mushíru'l-Mulk deputized his friend Hájí Siyyid Ismá'íl to attain the presence of Bahá'u'lláh and present to Him, on his behalf, the sum of one thousand túmáns and an exquisite pen-case. Bahá'u'lláh graciously accepted the pen-case but declined the money which He gave to the bearer. He revealed a Tablet for Mushíru'l-Mulk which was brought to Shíráz by Shaykh Salmán and delivered to him through his friend Hájí Siyyid Ismá'íl.

On hearing that Shaykh Salmán was in Shíráz, Mushíru'l-Mulk intimated his desire to meet him and asked his friend to bring Shaykh Salmán to his house the next day. But Shaykh Salmán did not wish to meet Mushíru'l-Mulk. He declined the invitation, giving the excuse that he had no time as he was in a hurry to leave Shíráz. Mushíru'l-Mulk, however, was very eager for this meeting and responded to this message by saying: 'Now that Shaykh Salmán is in such a hurry to go, I shall come instead to his place of residence in the morning.'

When this message was conveyed to Shaykh Salmán he turned to me and said, 'Let us collect our belongings and leave this place.' We left the home of Hájí Siyyid Ismá'íl and took residence in a caravanserai in the town.

Hájí Siyyid Ismá'íl could not understand Shaykh Salmán's reason for refusing to meet Mushíru'l-Mulk and begged him to change his mind. But he refused, saying: 'If Mushíru'l-Mulk meets me he will lose his faith and will leave the Cause. When pressed to give his reasons Shaykh Salmán replied, 'Mushíru'l-Mulk has heard many traditions and stories

[12] A civil dignitary.

> about Salmán, the disciple of Muḥammad. For instance, he has heard the fantastic story that fire had no effect upon the feet of Salmán, and that he used to put his own feet instead of wood into a fireplace and heat the pots up with them. No doubt, Mushíru'l-Mulk expects to see similar things from me or he thinks that I have a face radiant and beautiful as an angel's. When he sees my ugly face and rough appearance he will leave the Faith.' Later on this story was mentioned to Bahá'u'lláh, Who confirmed that Shaykh Salmán had been right and that Mushíru'l-Mulk would have left the Faith had that meeting taken place. [13]

As we have seen earlier, Shaykh Salmán, in spite of his little knowledge, was possessed of a shrewd judgment and a fine spiritual perception. For instance, Bahá'u'lláh's Tablets did not usually bear the name of the recipient because of the danger of identifying local believers if the documents reached the hands of the authorities. This posed a problem to Shaykh Salmán as to whom each Tablet was to be delivered. To make things more difficult he was illiterate and therefore not able to read the content. However, his spiritual insight was so great that he would ask another believer to read the content and based on the content and the tone of the Blessed Beauty's words he would allocate the Tablet to its correct recipient. Then Shaykh Salmán would ask another believer to write the name on the Tablet for its delivery.

'Abdu'l-Bahá wrote: "From the dawn of history until the present day, there has never been a messenger so worthy of trust; there has never been a courier to compare with Salmán ... Upon him be the glory of God, the All-Glorious; unto him be salutations and praise.." [14]

2. "The Bábí-Maker"

There were other facets of the character of Shaykh Salmán that made him unforgettable. Among them was his zeal for teaching the Faith.

---

[13]Adib Taherzadeh. *The Revelation of Bahá'u'lláh,* vol 1. George Ronald Oxford, 1974, pp. 111-112.

[14]Abdu'l-Bahá. *Memorials of the Faithful.* Wilmette, Bahá'í Publishing Trust, 1971, p.15.

'Abdu'l-Bahá once remarked: "The Blessed Beauty named Shaykh Salmán a 'Bábí-maker', for whenever he returned from a journey to Iran he used to submit a long list of newly declared believers and ask that Tablets might be revealed in their honour".[15] Also, his Muslim friends referred to him as the "the Bábís' Angel Gabriel" (Jabrá'íl-i Bábíyan). [16,17]

2.1 Saved by the Providence

In his book *Memorials of the Faithful* 'Abdu'l-Bahá tells of one of the many moments of difficulty in which Providence helped Shaykh Salmán.

> One day, Shaykh Salmán being a Bábí [18], was passing through a bazaar in the city of Tehran accompanied by one of the believers. The guards and police followed him and discovered where he lived. In those times of persecution, a Bábí could be arrested under the sole accusation of professing the Faith of the Báb. The next day, a group of gendarmes returned and arrested him taking him to the police head.
>
> "Who are you?" the chief asked.
>
> "I am from Hindíyán," replied Salmán. "I have come to Ṭihrán and am on my way to Khurásán, for a pilgrimage to the Shrine of Imám Riḍá."
>
> "What were you doing yesterday," the chief asked, "with that man in the white robe?"
>
> Salmán answered, "I had sold him an 'abá the day before, and yesterday he was to pay me."
>
> "You are a stranger here," the chief said. "How could you trust him?"
>
> "A money-changer guaranteed the payment," Salmán replied.

---

[15]Youness Afroukhteh. *Memories of Nine Years in 'Akká* (translated by Riaz Masrour). George Ronald Oxford, 2004, p.228

[16]'Abdu'l-Bahá. *Memorials of the Faithful.* Wilmette, Bahá'í Publishing Trust, 1971, pp.15.

[17]Moojan Momen. *The Bahá'í Communities of Iran.* George Ronald, 2015, p. 176.

[18]A Bábí was a follower of the Faith of the Báb.

He had in mind the respected believer, Áqá Muḥammad-i-Sarráf (money-changer).

The chief turned to one of his farráshes [19]and said, "Take him to the money-changer's and look into it."

When they reached there the farrásh went on ahead.

"What was all this," he said, "about the sale of an 'abá[20] and your vouching for the payment? Explain yourself."

"I know nothing about it," the money-changer replied.

"Come along," said the farrásh to Salmán. "All is clear at last. You are a Bábí."

It happened that the turban which Salmán had on his head was similar to those worn in Shúshtar. As they were passing a crossroads, a man from Shúshtar came out of his shop.

He embraced Salmán and cried: "Where have you been, Khájíh Muḥammad-'Alí? When did you arrive? Welcome!"

Salmán replied, "I came here a few days ago and now the police have arrested me."

"What do you want with him?" the merchant asked the farrásh. "What are you after?"

"He is a Bábí," was the answer.

"God forbid!" cried the man from Shúshtar. "I know him well. Khájíh Muḥammad-'Alí is a God-fearing Muslim, a Shí'ih, a devout follower of the Imám 'Alí." With this he gave the farrásh a sum of money and Salmán was freed.

They went into the shop and the merchant began to ask Salmán how he was faring. Salmán told him: "I am not Khájíh Muḥammad-'Alí."

The man from Shúshtar was dumbfounded. "You look exactly like him!" he exclaimed. "You two are identical. However, since you are not he, give me back the money I paid the farrásh."

[19]Farrásh means an officer.

[20]An oriental long coat.

> Salmán immediately handed him the money, left, went out through the city gate and made for Hindíyán. [21]

2.2 A Person of Fine Judgment

Shaykh Salmán also had a great thirst for knowledge and easily understood questions of weight and depth. He used to ask some believers of great knowledge to explain some matters that he could not understand. When, however, he met with pretention or arrogance Shaykh Salmán sometimes struggled to manifest tact, or even courtesy. This occasionally caused problems for the Bahá'í community.

Hájí Mírzá Ḥaydar 'Alí, was an enlightened Bahá'í traveling teacher who came to be known by the appellation 'Angel of Carmel'. He wrote of his experience meeting Shaykh Salmán as follows:

> I spent some time in Shíráz where I used to attain the presence of the celebrated Salmán... I was filled with infinite joy by associating with him. He was truly a brilliant lamp. Outwardly he was an illiterate person and very simple, but inwardly he was the essence of wisdom and knowledge who could solve difficult problems and explain abstruse questions in simple language. Salmán was the essence of selflessness, he had no ego whatsoever. He was in no way able to flatter people or to deal deceitfully with them. It was for this reason that the pure in heart among the believers were truly devoted to him. But those who were sophisticated and conventional were not keen to associate with him. For they feared that he might ruin their prestige in the gatherings of the friends. It is commonly known and is true, that once the Ancient Beauty told Salmán to show respect towards important people in the meetings, and not to speak unkindly about them. Salmán replied, 'I do not consider anybody great except the Ancient Beauty and the Master. The so-called great are nothing but pompous men.' This remark amused Bahá'u'lláh. [22]

---

[21] 'Abdu'l-Bahá. *Memorials of the Faithful.* Wilmette, Bahá'í Publishing Trust, 1971, pp.13-14.

[22] Adib Taherzadeh. *The Revelation of Bahá'u'lláh,* vol 2. George Ronald Oxford, 1974, pp. 283-284.

As seen above, Bahá'u'lláh held Shaykh Salmán's judgement in high regard. "He was close to the heart of Bahá'u'lláh, Who looked upon him with especial favor and grace. Among the Holy Scriptures, there are Tablets revealed in his name", said 'Abdu'l-Bahá. [23]

According to Adib Taherzadeh

> Believers who wished to attain the presence of Bahá'u'lláh would seek permission from Him to do so, and in this matter Bahá'u'lláh relied so much on Shaykh Salmán's judgement that at one stage He delegated to him the authority to give permission, on His behalf, to those upon whom this great privilege was to be conferred. [24]

2.3 The Story of Muḥammad-Báqir-i-Qazvíní

At times during his travels throughout Iran as courier Shaykh Salmán was asked to carry monetary contributions towards the Head of the Faith in 'Akká:

> Hájí Muḥammad-Báqir-i-Qazvíní... had asked Bahá'u'lláh to be given wealth. In response, Bahá'u'lláh had said to Javád, "Write your brother that such a thing is not in his interest." Hájí Muḥammad-Baqir had asked a second time, and once again, Bahá'u'lláh had answered through Javád, "Write him that it is not in his interest." This time Hájí Muḥammad Báqir had written his brother, Javád, "Go and on my behalf and take hold of the hem of His blessed garment and tearfully supplicate wealth for me." This time Bahá'u'lláh had responded, "Jináb-i-Jud, even though it is not in his interest, We have bestowed it upon him. Write him to come to Istanbul and commence trading."
>
> [Hájí Muḥammad-Báqir did as bidden, and] since it was war time and the demand and price for the cotton goods had soared enormously, he became so engaged in this commerce and was profiting with such enormity that he had no time

[23]'Abdu'l-Bahá. *Memorials of the Faithful.* Wilmette, Bahá'í Publishing Trust, 1971, p.15.

[24]Adib Taherzadeh. *The Revelation of Bahá'u'lláh,* vol 1. George Ronald Oxford, 1974, pp. 111.

to even look after his daily accounts. It was about this time that the celebrated Shaykh Salmán arrived and he had with him a contribution from one of the believers in Iran in form of a check that needed to be cashed by Hájí Muḥammad-Báqir and the sum delivered to Bahá'u'lláh. Therefore, the Shaykh went to Hájí's place of business and presented this check. The Hájí responded, "I have no time now, return on the morrow." On the following day, inattentively, he repeated the same reply. This manner of treatment went on for a week until finally Shaykh Salmán protested, "Hájí, this is not mine, but God's money!" In response to which the Hájí had brought his fist down on his cash box and answered with pride and conceit, "My god is in this box!"

Having become enraged, the Shaykh, without cashing the check, left at once and proceeded to the Holy Land. On the first day of attaining the presence of Bahá'u'lláh, still being deeply angered by what had transpired, and with his customary dialect, he stated, "For forty years You have ruled as God, and yet, do not know upon whom You should bestow riches!" Bahá'u'lláh had smiled and said, "Jináb-i-Shaykh, what has happened?" After hearing the details from Salmán, Bahá'u'lláh had replied, "Be assured that the same God Who bestowed riches on him, can claim it back."

Before long, the above-mentioned Hájí became destitute to the point that he was bereft of the evening meal. [Abú'l-Qásim Afnán adds that he heard from his father, Mírzá Habíb, "Hájí Muḥammad-Báqir was in Cairo and to earn an income would sell wooden spoons for a small coin, but no one would buy any from him!"]. [25]

2.4 The Wedding of 'Abdu'l-Bahá

After a wave of hostilities arose in Shíráz in October 1846, the Blessed Báb was sent to the city of Iṣfahán. In that city He stayed for several months in an atmosphere of peace and tranquility until this period

[25]Mírzá Habíbu'lláh Afnán. *Memories of the Báb, Bahá'u'lláh and `Abdu'l-Bahá* (Translated and Annotated by Ahang Rabbani). An electronic-publication of Kalimat Press, 2005, pp. 204-206.

was interrupted and followed by a long and rigorous imprisonment in the mountains of Adhirbayjan.

In those days, several believers were blessed to be close to Him. Among them was Mírzá Ibráhím, whose brother, Mírzá Muḥammad 'Alí had not been able to have children during their marriage.

Once, during a meal in the house where the Báb was staying, Mírzá Ibráhím approached Him and explained his brother's case, asking Him for a special blessing so that the couple could have a child.

After listening to his plea, the Báb set aside a portion of his own food and asked that it be shared with the brother and his wife. Some time later a girl was born in that home, who was given the name of Fáṭimih, though Bahá'u'lláh later conferred upon her the name of Munírih (Illumined). She was chosen by Him to be the wife of His dear eldest Son, 'Abdu'l-Bahá.

In 1872 Shaykh Salmán was entrusted by Bahá'u'lláh with a special mission. He was to take Fátimih from Isfahan to 'Akká for her wedding to 'Abdu'l-Bahá. Upon his arrival he went to see a faithful believer who was later martyred and given the title "The King of Martyrs". This man was Munírih's cousin.

"I have brought you tidings of a wonderful bounty," he said. "I am commissioned to take your cousin, the daughter of the late Mírzá Muḥammad-'Alí, to the Holy Land, going by way of Mecca as pilgrims on *ḥajj* [26]. You must make arrangements for us to leave Isfahán in time for the pilgrimage, to travel to Shíraz and Búshihr. These preparations must be done quietly, and no one should know of our journey until a few days before our departure." [27]

Preparations were made and the day of departure arrived. Shaykh Salmán travelled with Munírih Khánum, her brother and a servant. They all departed for Shíráz — a city 500 km away. Arriving in that city, they took lodging in an inn, but members of the Báb's family soon arrived to receive them. The group then accepted the invitation to move to the family home. At that time, the Báb's widow was alive

[26]Hajj means pilgrimage.

[27]Hasan Balyuzi. *Bahá'u'lláh, the King of Glory.* George Ronald Oxford, 1991, pp. 344.

in Shíráz.

From Shíráz they went to the port of Búshihr and then by sea to Mecca, where they arrived in February 1873. Detailed instructions for this long, arduous and risky journey, had been provided by Bahá'u'lláh to Shaykh Salmán.

After visiting the sacred city of the Muslims, the group returned to the port of Jiddah where they found that a telegram from Bahá'u'lláh's amanuensis had arrived. In the communication they were advised to wait for a while until the pilgrims from Mecca had left Arabia. When this happened, they were to continue the journey to Alexandria in Egypt and wait there for another telegram from the Holy Land containing new instructions. The reason for this change in plan was that the conditions of Bahá'u'lláh's confinement had intensified in the prison city of 'Akká.

In Jiddah they were subject to much suspicion on the part of the Muslims and therefore they were in a very dangerous situation. They later embarked for Alexandria where they met seventeen Bahá'ís. Finally, a telegram arrived from Bahá'u'lláh allowing them to go to the prison city, crossing the Mediterranean Sea by ship.

Their arrival at the port of 'Akká' occurred in the darkness of the night. As per the instructions, they did not disembark until a believer received them. They waited until a Bahá'í came in a small boat shouting "Shaykh Salmán, Shaykh Salmán".

In this way, Salmán fulfilled this delicate mission entrusted by his Lord. The next day, Shaykh Salmán, Munírih Khánum, Mírzá Ibráhím and the servant who accompanied them were taken to the presence of Bahá'u'lláh. The first words of the Blessed Beauty were: '"We brought you into the prison-city, at a time when the prison-gates were closed in the face of all, to make clear and evident to all the power of God." [28]

The wedding between 'Abdu'l-Bahá and Munírih Khánum took place after five months. Financial challenges made it difficult to secure a place for the new couple, which caused the delay. The description of such a memorable event was left to posterity by Munírih Khánum herself:

---

[28]Hasan Balyuzi. *Bahá'u'lláh, the King of Glory*. George Ronald Oxford, 1991, pp. 348.

Then the night of union, preferable to a hundred thousand years, drew nigh. I was dressed in a white robe which had been prepared for me by the fingers of the Greatest Holy Leaf, and which was more precious than the silks and velvets of Paradise. About nine o'clock in the evening, the soul-ravishing voice of the Peerless Beloved was heard from the Supreme Concourse, and I was permitted to stand in the Presence of Bahá'u'lláh. Attended by the Greatest Holy Leaf, I listened to the words of the Blessed Perfection, who was resting under a mosquito net. He said:

"You are welcome! You are welcome! O thou my Blessed Leaf and Maid Servant! We have chosen thee and accepted thee to be the companion of the Greatest Branch and to serve him. This is from My Bounty, to which there is no equal; the treasures of the earth and heaven cannot be compared with it."

After speaking in this manner, and showering His Mercy upon me, he referred to Baghdad, Adrianople and the Most Great Prison, saying that many girls had hoped for this great bounty, but they were not accepted.

"Thou must be very thankful for thou has attained to this most great favor and bestowal."

Bahá'u'lláh then sent us away with the words:

"May you always be under the Protection of God."

You can easily imagine, after listening to these heavenly words, and beholding these lordly bestowals, in what glorious atmosphere I was soaring. How marvelously had all my hopes been fulfilled. As the Persian Poet says:

"At that moment the heaven, addressing the earth declares, 'If thou hast not seen the resurrection with thine own eyes, come and behold!'"

After that blessed hour and fortunate time, I dwelt in the paradise of eternity with a world of longing, attraction, humility and submission. I entered the room prepared for the Greatest Branch and experienced his favor, his affection, his glory and his grandeur.

An hour later, 'Abdul-Bahá, the wife of Kalím[29], the wife of Khojeh Abboud, the owner of the house, and his daughter entered the room. The mother of Mírzá Muḥammad Alí brought with her the special Tablets which are read and chanted on such occasions, especially that Tablet of Bahá'u'lláh which begins with the joyous declaration:

"Verily the doors of Paradise are opened and the divine Youth hath appeared!"

She delivered this Tablet to me and besought me to chant. Involuntarily I took that blessed Tablet into my hands and began to chant with a clear and resonant voice. In later years, whenever I would meet the wife of Abboud, she would refer to that night, saying she could not forget that meeting, and the sweetness of that chanting was still ringing in her ears. She would say: "Never before in this world, have I heard a bride chanting at her own wedding." [30]

3. The Pen of the Blessed Beauty Addresses Salmán

Bahá'u'lláh revealed at least three Tablets for Shaykh Salmán. These have been partially translated by the Guardian and appear in the book *Gleanings from the Writings of Bahá'u'lláh* [31] and *The Promised Day Is Come* [32].

The first Tablet is called Madínatu't-Tawḥíd (The City of the Unity of God). It was revealed in Baghdád in response to Shaykh Salmán's question on the meaning of the "Unity of God", a theme that among the theologians themselves provoked intense and long discussions. Its English translation is published in *Gleanings from the Writings of Bahá'u'lláh,* section XXIV. It contains explanations of high mystical content in the very rich and expressive Arabic language.

[29]Mírzá Musá, Bahá'u'lláh's brother.

[30]Munírih Khánum. *Episodes in the Life of Munírih Khánum* (translated by Mirza Ahmad Sohrab.) Los Angeles: Persian American Publishing Company, 1924.

[31]Bahá'u'lláh. *Gleanings from the Writings of Bahá'u'lláh.* US Bahá'í Publishing Trust, 1990.

[32]Shoghi Effendi. *The Promised Day Is Come.* US Bahá'í Publishing Trust, 1980.

The second Tablet was revealed in Adrianople and is described by the Guardian as one of the "most significant among Bahá'u'lláh's Writings" [33]. It was revealed primarily in Persian, comprises about thirty pages, and its English translation is included in *Gleanings from the Writings of Bahá'u'lláh*, sections XXI, CXLVIII and CLIV.

According to Iraj Ayman, [34] some themes expounded in this second Tablet include:

- The Words of God are sealed treasuries of divine knowledge
- The letters of negation which preceded the letters of affirmation are now eliminated
- The Bahá'í concept of the relationship between the Creator and humankind
- The Will of God is all encompassing
- The significance of the names and attributes in the realm of God and in the world of creation
- Bahá'í interpretation of reunion with God and the concepts of unity and diversity
- The nature of belief and disbelief.

There is also a third Tablet revealed in 'Akká, a small paragraph of which was translated by the Guardian in "The Promised Day Is Come". [35] Extracts from these Tablets are reproduced below.

3.1 Tablet of Salmán I (Revealed in Ba<u>gh</u>dád) [36]

Beware, O believers in the Unity of God, lest ye be tempted to make any distinction between any of the Manifestations of His Cause, or to discriminate against the signs that have accompanied and proclaimed their Revelation. This indeed is the true meaning of Divine Unity, if ye be of them that apprehend and believe this truth. Be ye assured,

---

[33]Adib Taherzadeh. *The Revelation of Bahá'u'lláh.* Oxford, U. K.: George Ronald, 1977, Vol. 1, p. 283.

[34]Iraj Ayman. *Principles of Bahá'í Theology in the Tablet of Salmán.* Paper presented at the Irfan Colloquia. Louhelen Bahá'í School, Michigan, October 9-12, 1988.

[35]Shoghi Effendi. *The Promised Day Is Come.* US Bahá'í Publishing Trust, 1980.

[36]This Tablet is known as Madínatu't-Tawḥíd (The City of the Unity of God).

moreover, that the works and acts of each and every one of these Manifestations of God, nay whatever pertaineth unto them, and whatsoever they may manifest in the future, are all ordained by God, and are a reflection of His Will and Purpose. Whoso maketh the slightest possible difference between their persons, their words, their messages, their acts and manners, hath indeed disbelieved in God, hath repudiated His signs, and betrayed the Cause of His Messengers.[37]

3.2 Tablet of Salmán II (Revealed in Adrianople)

O Salmán! The door of the knowledge of the Ancient Being hath ever been, and will continue for ever to be, closed in the face of men. No man's understanding shall ever gain access unto His holy court. As a token of His mercy, however, and as a proof of His loving-kindness, He hath manifested unto men the Day Stars of His divine guidance, the Symbols of His divine unity, and hath ordained the knowledge of these sanctified Beings to be identical with the knowledge of His own Self. Whoso recognizeth them hath recognized God. Whoso hearkeneth to their call, hath hearkened to the Voice of God, and whoso testifieth to the truth of their Revelation, hath testified to the truth of God Himself. Whoso turneth away from them, hath turned away from God, and whoso disbelieveth in them, hath disbelieved in God. Every one of them is the Way of God that connecteth this world with the realms above, and the Standard of His Truth unto every one in the kingdoms of earth and heaven. They are the Manifestations of God amidst men, the evidences of His Truth, and the signs of His glory.[38]

O Salmán! All that the sages and mystics have said or written have never exceeded, nor can they ever hope to exceed, the limitations to which man's finite mind hath been strictly subjected. To whatever heights the mind of the most exalted of men may soar, however great the depths which the detached and understanding heart can penetrate, such mind and heart can never transcend that which is the creature of their own conceptions and the product of their own thoughts. The meditations of the profoundest thinker, the devotions of the holiest

[37]Bahá'u'lláh. *Gleanings from the Writings of Bahá'u'lláh* (XXIV). US Bahá'í Publishing Trust, pp. 59, 1990.

[38]Bahá'u'lláh. *Gleanings from the Writings of Bahá'u'lláh* (XXI). US Bahá'í Publishing Trust, pp. 49-50, 1990.

of saints, the highest expressions of praise from either human pen or tongue, are but a reflection of that which hath been created within themselves, through the revelation of the Lord, their God. Whoever pondereth this truth in his heart will readily admit that there are certain limits which no human being can possibly transgress. Every attempt which, from the beginning that hath no beginning, hath been made to visualize and know God is limited by the exigencies of His own creation—a creation which He, through the operation of His own Will and for the purposes of none other but His own Self, hath called into being. Immeasurably exalted is He above the strivings of human mind to grasp His Essence, or of human tongue to describe His mystery. No tie of direct intercourse can ever bind Him to the things He hath created, nor can the most abstruse and most remote allusions of His creatures do justice to His being. Through His world-pervading Will He hath brought into being all created things. He is and hath ever been veiled in the ancient eternity of His own exalted and indivisible Essence, and will everlastingly continue to remain concealed in His inaccessible majesty and glory. All that is in heaven and all that is in the earth have come to exist at His bidding, and by His Will all have stepped out of utter nothingness into the realm of being. How can, therefore, the creature which the Word of God hath fashioned comprehend the nature of Him Who is the Ancient of Days? [39]

Warn, O Salmán, the beloved of the one true God, not to view with too critical an eye the sayings and writings of men. Let them rather approach such sayings and writings in a spirit of open-mindedness and loving sympathy. Those men, however, who, in this Day, have been led to assail, in their inflammatory writings, the tenets of the Cause of God, are to be treated differently. It is incumbent upon all men, each according to his ability, to refute the arguments of those that have attacked the Faith of God. Thus hath it been decreed by Him Who is the All-Powerful, the Almighty. He that wisheth to promote the Cause of the one true God, let him promote it through his pen and tongue, rather than have recourse to sword or violence. We have, on a previous occasion, revealed this injunction, and We now confirm it, if ye be of them that comprehend. By the righteousness of Him

[39]Bahá'u'lláh. *Gleanings from the Writings of Bahá'u'lláh (CXLVIII).* US Bahá'í Publishing Trust, p. 316-317, 1990.

Who, in this Day, crieth within the inmost heart of all created things: "God, there is none other God besides Me!" If any man were to arise to defend, in his writings, the Cause of God against its assailants, such a man, however inconsiderable his share, shall be so honored in the world to come that the Concourse on high would envy his glory. No pen can depict the loftiness of his station, neither can any tongue describe its splendor. For whosoever standeth firm and steadfast in this holy, this glorious, and exalted Revelation, such power shall be given him as to enable him to face and withstand all that is in heaven and on earth. Of this God is Himself a witness.

O ye beloved of God! Repose not yourselves on your couches, nay bestir yourselves as soon as ye recognize your Lord, the Creator, and hear of the things which have befallen Him, and hasten to His assistance. Unloose your tongues, and proclaim unceasingly His Cause. This shall be better for you than all the treasures of the past and of the future, if ye be of them that comprehend this truth. [40]

3.3 Tablet of Salmán III (Revealed in 'Akká)

One of the signs of the maturity of the world is that no one will accept to bear the weight of kingship. Kingship will remain with none willing to bear alone its weight. That day will be the day whereon wisdom will be manifested among mankind. Only in order to proclaim the Cause of God and spread abroad His Faith will anyone be willing to bear this grievous weight. Well is it with him who, for love of God and His Cause, and for the sake of God and for the purpose of proclaiming His Faith, will expose himself unto this great danger, and will accept this toil and trouble.[41]

4. An Explanation of the Tablet to Salmán Revealed in Adrianople - by Adib Taherzadeh

In the *Tablet of Salmán* Bahá'u'lláh bids him to journey throughout the land with feet of steadfastness, wings of detachment and a heart ablaze with the fire of the love of God, so that the forces of evil may be powerless to prevent him from carrying out his mission.

---

[40]Bahá'u'lláh. *Gleanings from the Writings of Bahá'u'lláh (CLIV).* US Bahá'í Publishing Trust, p. 328-329, 1990.

[41]Shoghi Effendi. *The Promised Day Is Come.* US Bahá'í Publishing Trust, 1980, p. 70.

Revealed at the time when Mírzá Yaḥyá had openly arisen against Bahá'u'lláh, this Tablet also contains many passages concerning the unfaithfulness, the treachery, the ungodliness of Mírzá Yaḥyá and his shameful activities including his plans to take the life of Bahá'u'lláh. In moving language, He pours out His heart to Salmán and speaks of the anguish of His own heart, of His pains and sufferings which were inflicted by one whom He had brought up with such loving-kindness, care and consideration. He recalls the times when Mírzá Yaḥyá was in constant attendance by day and night. He would stand humbly in His presence and listen to the Words of God which were revealed with great power and majesty. But as the Cause began to grow, he was enticed by the prospect of his own fame. His whole being was so filled with the love of leadership that he left his Lord and rebelled against Him. Bahá'u'lláh in this Tablet intimates to Shaykh Salmán that He is so encompassed by grief and sorrow that His Pen is prevented from bestowing the knowledge of God upon people and revealing some of the mysteries of His Cause.

A great part of the *Tablet of Salmán* is in answer to a question concerning the meaning of a line from a poem by Mawlaví. [42] In order to appreciate Baháu'lláh's profound explanations, one must be well versed in Islamic philosophy and the meaning of mystical terms. Otherwise it is not an easy task to understand this part of the Tablet. Furthermore, Bahá'u'lláh states that He is reluctant to expound the works of the mystics and sages of the past. For, He proclaims, the Sun of Truth has risen and oceans of knowledge have surged forth through His Revelation. Therefore there is no need to dwell on the words and teachings of old. Gnostics and men of learning must needs turn to Him as the source of knowledge and receive enlightenment from Him.

Bahá'u'lláh calls on Salmán to meet the servants of God and counsel them on His behalf. They should cleanse their hearts so that they may be enabled to recognize the Beauty of His countenance, walk in His ways, meditate upon His Words, and know that if the worlds of God were limited to this one, the Báb would never have allowed Himself to fall into the hands of His enemy, nor would He have sacrificed His life in the path of God. In another Tablet Bahá'u'lláh states that if there were any merit in this mortal world, He Himself would have occupied

[42]A famous Persian poet.

its highest thrones and owned all its treasures. The fact that the Creator of this world has not set His own affection upon it is a proof that there are spiritual worlds far more glorious than this one. It is to these worlds that the soul of the believer repairs after its separation from the body.

Bahá'u'lláh in the *Tablet of Salmán* promises that through the influence of His Revelation, some souls will arise who, renouncing the world, will turn fully to Him with the utmost devotion, and regard the sacrifice of life in His path as the easiest of all things. He affirms that God has chosen these souls for His own Self, and that the dwellers of the realms on high long to attain their presence.

The history of the Cause records with pride many episodes in the lives of such believers, who have shed a great lustre upon the Faith of Bahá'u'lláh. The tree of the Cause of God in this day has grown and flourished mainly as a result of two factors: one, the outpouring of the Revelation of Bahá'u'lláh which, like the rays of the sun, has imparted to it a measure of its vivifying energies; the other, the blood of the martyrs who willingly gave their lives in order to nourish and water it.

Bahá'u'lláh in this Tablet confers an exalted station upon the soul of the believer. He states that if the glory of such a station be revealed in this world, even to the extent of a needle's eye, every soul will expire through ecstasy. Because of this, the station of the true believer is kept hidden in this life.

In the *Tablet of Salmán* Bahá'u'lláh explains one of the most interesting mysteries in the *Qur'án,* a mystery which had hitherto remained unnoticed. He refers to the well-known phrase, 'There is no God but Him'. This is the cardinal statement of faith which every Muslim must make, and which is the basis of the Islamic religion.

As we have previously written, the Word of God has many significances which are beyond the ken of men. There are inner meanings enshrined in the Word of God which only His Manifestation and those whom He guides understand. Bahá'u'lláh explains that in this phrase 'There is no God but Him', the letter of negation precedes that of affirmation. Therefore as a result of the creative influence of this phrase, ever since it was revealed, the violators of the Cause of

God, representing the letter of negation, dominated over the faithful in the past. All the sufferings which the hands of the breakers of the Covenant of God inflicted upon the steadfast Muslims and their apparent superiority, were the fulfilment of the Words uttered by Muḥammad. God had, through His wisdom, so destined that those who were impure and rebellious should dominate those who were true and sincere.

It is a Bahá'í belief that those who usurped the right of Imám 'Alí, the lawful successor of Muḥammad and the interpreter of His Word, were acting against the expressed wishes of their Prophet. They disregarded the injunctions of Muḥammad concerning His successor, became the primary cause of division within the Faith of Islám, brought about the death of the holy Imáms and persecuted their followers. They were the letters of negation and till the end of the Dispensation of Muḥammad, dominated His faithful followers.

History demonstrates that great differences arose among the followers of each religion soon after the death of its Founder. These differences led to schisms and divisions which have increased with the passage of time. This process, however, must not be so misunderstood as to lead us to believe that the Founders of the world's great religions in the past were incapable of establishing ways and means of uniting their followers, or of staying the hands of the unfaithful from corrupting the religion of God.

That religions have divided into sects is not due to the teachings of their Founders, but rather to the immaturity of their followers. Just as children are too young to be held responsible for keeping their clothes clean as they play outside, so humanity in past dispensations had not acquired sufficient maturity to protect the religion of God from disunity and discord.

Even in Islám, the most recent of the older religions, men were not sufficiently mature to receive from Muḥammad a firm Covenant, similar to that established by Bahá'u'lláh, a Covenant which would require His followers strictly to follow His Faith without creating division within it. On the contrary, as we have already observed from the fore-mentioned phrase in the Qur'án, Muḥammad knew that His followers would not be capable of maintaining their unity after Him. He knew that if He were to establish an irrevocable covenant in writing, the people of Islám would not have had the maturity and capacity at that time to observe its provisions strictly. But this is not to be regarded as a failure on the part of Islám, or of older religions which became similarly divided. It was only natural for humanity, which had not come of age, to neglect its duty and conduct itself irresponsibly. However, through God's forbearance and justice, the followers of past religions received their spiritual sustenance regardless of the sects they created.

For example, the primacy of Peter is acknowledged in the Gospels. However, differences arose and the followers of Christ became divided. Nevertheless each sect received a measure of the bounties of Christ. The tree of Christianity blossomed even after acquiring several branches, and each one remained verdant and flourishing until the advent of Islám when the Dispensation of Christ was closed. Similarly, the two major branches of Islám remained part of that religion. Even those who violated the wishes of the Prophet were not cut off from the Tree of Islám; all received their sustenance from it until the advent of the Báb when the Dispensation of Islám came to an end.

However, the Dispensation of Bahá'u'lláh has ushered in a new day. Through the potency of His Revelation mankind is destined to come of age and Bahá'u'lláh has given it responsibility. He established an irrefutable Covenant with His followers, appointed its Centre, 'Abdu'l-Bahá, exhorted the believers to follow Him and made it clear that in this Dispensation there would be no room for disunity and division. The Cause of God is one and indivisible, and man, having left behind the stages of childhood and adolescence, must now play a responsible part in maintaining its unity, in consolidating its world-wide structure and in protecting its nascent institutions from the unfaithful.

Referring to the fore-mentioned phrase 'There is no God but Him', Bahá'u'lláh, in the *Tablet of Salmán*, proclaims in majestic and powerful language that He has removed the letter of negation which had been placed before that of affirmation. This phrase, which the Prophet of Islám, through His all-encompassing wisdom, regarded to be the cornerstone of His Faith, is now, in the Dispensation of Bahá'u'lláh, symbolically replaced by the affirmative phrase 'He is God', signifying that the Revealer of the Cause of God holds within His hands the reins of authority, and, unlike the Dispensations of the past, no one has the power to wrest it from Him. The violators and the breakers of Bahá'u'lláh's Covenant, as history has shown, have been utterly impotent to introduce divisions within His Faith, to arrest its onward march or influence its glorious destiny... [43]

[43]Adib Taherzadeh. *The Revelation of Bahá'u'lláh*. Oxford, U. K.: George Ronald, 1977, Vol. 2, p. 284-289.

Figure 1: Shaykh Salmán. Courtesy: Bahá'í Media

Figure 2: The land gate of 'Akká from inside the city.
Courtesy: Bahá'í Media

Figure 3: The barracks in 'Akka were Bahá'u'lláh was imprisoned.
Courtesy: Bahá'í Media

Figure 4: Bahá'u'lláh's cell in the Prison of 'Akká.
Courtesy: Bahá'í Media

Figure 5: Map of Irán.
Courtesy: Pedro Donaires

Figure 6: Nabíl-i-A'ẓam

Figure 7: Bahá'ís in Adrianople.
Courtesy: Bahá'í Media

YÁR-MUḤAMMAD-I-ZARANDÍ

ENTITLED
NABÍL-I-A'ẒAM - THE GREATEST WISE -

"THE LAUREATE POET, CHRONICLER AND INDEFATIGABLE DISCIPLE OF BAHÁ'U'LLÁH"

By God, though weariness should weaken Me, and hunger should destroy Me, though My couch should be made of the hard rock and My associates of the beasts of the desert, I will not blench, but will be patient, as the resolute and determined are patient, in the strength of God, the King of Preexistence, the Creator of the nations; and under all circumstances I give thanks unto God.

Bahá'u'lláh[44]

[44]'Abdu'l-Bahá. *A Traveler's Narrative.* US Bahá'í Publishing Trust, 1980, p. 80.

Nabíl-i-A'ẓam

1. Nabíl the Scholar

This is the story of Yár Muḥammad, a simple shepherd who became Nabíl-i-A'ẓam, in Arabic, the *Greatest Nobleman* of the Bahá'í Faith. Nabíl-i-A'ẓam may well be called the father of Bahá'í historians. He was a key chronicler of Bábí and early Bahá'í history. He had ready access to this history as he had the privilege to devotedly serve the Faith from its beginning. Because of his genuine, constant devotion and dedicated service rendered to Blessed Beauty, Nabíl was considered by Shoghi Effendi as one of the Nineteen Apostles of Bahá'u'lláh.

This chapter will start by describing his achievements as a historian and poet. This will be followed by an account of his initiation and services to the Cause. The last section presents a number of Tablets revealed by Bahá'u'lláh in his honour.

1.1 The Chronicler

Being a witness, participant and active researcher of the main events of the Cause of God, Nabíl resolved to document these events. This writing was published and widely read over many decades as *Nabíl's Narrative. Nabíl's Narrative* has acquired historical value of great magnitude, and is key reading for those who wish to deepen their knowledge on the history of the early days of the Faith.

The first of the two parts of the Narrative was translated by the beloved Guardian and was copiously annotated. The book, replete with illustrative photographs, was published in English in 1932 in the United States with the title The Dawn-Breakers. It documents the teachings and activities of Shaykh Aḥmad and Siyyid Káẓim; includes the Mission Statement of the Báb; records the conversion of Bahá'u'lláh and His first activities; describes the tragic scenes of the sites of Mázindarán, Nayríz and Zanján; and recounts in detail the life of the Báb until His public execution. This volume of twenty-six chapters ends with a description of the imprisonment of Bahá'u'lláh in Tehran and of His first exile to 'Iráq. *The Dawn-Breakers* has been published in several languages including Spanish, French, Dutch, Turkish, Hindi and German. It serves as a key text and source of inspiration for Bahá'ís around of the world.

The second volume is as yet unpublished. It provides a vivid chronicle of the life of the Blessed Beauty. Some passages of this portion of the history of the Faith have been translated by the beloved Guardian, Shoghi Effendi and are included in his history of the first century of the Bahá'í Faith, *God Passes By*.

The stories described in the narrative were in many cases observed by Nabíl himself. Where he recounted an incident to which he was not a witness, he took care to ensure the source was reliable. He quotes sources carefully, so as to preserve fidelity and authenticity. This is an important characteristic of this text which renders it superior over other contemporaneous stories, often distorted by oral tradition or reliant on secondary sources. One source of material for his narrative were reports and written accounts sent from Persia to Bahá'u'lláh in 'Akká. While in 'Akká, where he spent the last thirteen years of his life, Nabíl managed to interview veteran believers and pilgrims with whom he associated while living in the Holy Land. Currently, his work is an essential source for any historian and scholar of the Faith.

In the preface to his work, he makes the following statement:

> In certain instances I shall go into some detail, in others I shall content myself with a brief summary of events. I shall place on record a description of the episodes I myself have witnessed, as well as those that have been reported to me by trustworthy and recognised informants, specifying in every case their names and standing. Those to whom I am primarily indebted are the following: Mírzá Aḥmad-i-Qazvíní, the Báb's amanuensis; Siyyid Ismá'íl-i-Dhabíh; Shaykh Ḥasan-i-Zunúzí; Shaykh Abú-Turáb-i-Qazvíní; and, last but not least, Mírzá Músá, Áqáy-i-Kalím, brother of Bahá'u'lláh. [45]

Nabíl began writing his monumental work around the years 1887 and 1888, while in the Holy Land. He spent a year and a half completing it. He was assisted by Áqáy-i-Kalím, brother of Bahá'u'lláh. The first

[45]Nabíl. *The Dawn-Breakers: Nabíl's Narrative of the Early Days of the Bahá'í Revelation*. US Bahá'í Publishing Trust, 1932, p. lxiii.

passages were revised by Bahá'u'lláh through His amanuensis Mírzá Áqá Ján. Others were sighted by 'Abdu'l-Bahá.

"How abundantly", Nabíl thus describes his feelings after submitting a section of his Narrative to Bahá'u'lláh for review, "have my labours been rewarded by Him whose favour alone I seek, and for whose satisfaction I have addressed myself to this task! He graciously summoned me to His presence and vouchsafed me His blessings. I was in my home in the prison-city of 'Akká, and lived in the neighbourhood of the house of Áqáy-i-Kalím, when the summons of my Beloved reached me. That day [11 December 1888] I shall never forget". [46]

The period documented in the Narrative coincides with the forty-five year period of Nabíl's service to the Cause of God (1847-1892). Nabíl's prose is powerful and convincing. As a scholar he wrote with clarity and precision but his participation in the events he describes infused his writing with passion. He was aware that he was passing on a message that would transform people in centuries to come: "Whatever my pen has failed to record, future generations will, I hope, gather together and preserve for posterity." [47] Certainly, it is thanks to him that those events of incalculable spiritual and historical value have not been lost. With humility he acknowledged the limitations of his work:

> Many, I confess, are the gaps in this narrative, for which I beg the indulgence of my readers. It is my earnest hope that these gaps may be filled by those who will, after me, arise to compile an exhaustive and befitting account of these stirring events, the significance of which we can as yet but dimly discern. [48]

A careful study of the pages of his *Narrative*, makes it clear that Nabíl perceived the historical and spiritual significance of each event he recorded. His writing is emotionally charged and brings vividly to

---

[46] Nabíl. *The Dawn-Breakers: Nabíl's Narrative of the Early Days of the Bahá'í Revelation.* US Bahá'í Publishing Trust, 1932, p. 459.

[47] Nabíl. *The Dawn-Breakers: Nabíl's Narrative of the Early Days of the Bahá'í Revelation.* US Bahá'í Publishing Trust, 1932, pp. 581-582.

[48] Nabíl. *The Dawn-Breakers: Nabíl's Narrative of the Early Days of the Bahá'í Revelation.* US Bahá'í Publishing Trust, 1932, pp. 581-582.

life the episodes he recreates on paper. His mastery of language and the penetrating spirit that pervaded his pen, transports readers back to the past and allows them to experience those bygone moments. With grace and style Nabíl achieved many literary fronts: He liberates his audience from time and place and allows them to fly back in time. Thus the heroes, martyrs and saints of his Narrative live forever. Many of the people about whom he wrote were his close friends whose passing he dearly missed. Thus his prose is intensely human, as if the author is talking directly to one's heart. He is indeed the most powerful character within the Narrative reading the scene and telling us each story with charm.

For example, in the following passage describing Bahá'u'lláh's response in 1844 to the Message of the Báb, Nabíl captured the impression caused on the Báb in this eloquent manner:

> He [The Báb] felt assured that if now He were to fall suddenly a victim to the tyranny of His foes and depart from this world, the Cause which He had revealed would live; would, under the direction of Bahá'u'lláh, continue to develop and flourish, and would yield eventually its choicest fruit. The master-hand of Bahá'u'lláh would steer its course, and the pervading influence of His love would establish it in the hearts of men. Such a conviction fortified His spirit and filled Him with hope. From that moment His fears of the imminence of peril or danger entirely forsook Him. Phoenix-like He welcomed with joy the fire of adversity, and gloried in the glow and heat of its flame. [49]

Inspiring passages like these are discovered throughout the Narrative enlightening the soul and imparting certitude to the heart.

1.2 A Laureate Poet

Nabíl was also a consummated poet. A famous English writer called him Bahá'u'lláh's Poet-Laureate.[50] Many were the pilgrims to the Holy

[49]Nabíl. *The Dawn-Breakers: Nabíl's Narrative of the Early Days of the Bahá'í Revelation.* US Bahá'í Publishing Trust, 1932, p. 127.

[50]The writer is Edwards Granville Brown. Cf. Shoghi Effendi. *God Passes By*. US Bahá'í Publishing Trust, 1979, p.130.

Land who at the time of the Manifestation of God remembered him as one who cheered their days with the recitation of beautiful and inspiring mystical poems that he himself had composed.

Nabíl possessed a special gift and ultimately created a vast body of literature. Much of his free time was spent writing poems and odes dedicated to his Lord, Bahá'u'lláh. He often presented them in the form of a pentagon or hexagon. Nabíl shared his poetry with the rest of the believers who recognized the beauty and depth of the mysticism of these works. He gathered the believers in groups and sang the verses to them.

Nabíl composed several collections of poems in couplet form which is known in Persian as Mathnaví, but he also wrote in a variety of other styles. He wrote a set of poems after observing the pilgrimage to the House of the Báb in Shíráz, which he completed following Bahá'u'lláh's instructions. He also composed mathnavis describing the history of the Faith at various stages.[51,52] Nabíl also wrote treatises about the Bahá'í inheritance laws and the Badí calendar.[53] Various mathnavis have been published in both the East[54] and the West[55] though not all his poetry has been published.

'Abdu'l-Bahá, whom Nabíl loved very much, said of him that "He was a gifted poet, and his tongue most eloquent; a man of mettle, and on fire with passionate love" [56]... "His native genius was pure

[51]Frank Lewis. *Poetry as Revelation: Introduction to Bahá'u'lláh's 'Mathnavíy-i Mubárak'.* Published in Bahá'í *Studies Review,* 9. London: Association for Bahá'í Studies English-Speaking Europe, 1999. Available on: https://bahai-library.com/lewis_poetry_revelation

[52]Vahid Rafati. NABIL-E AʿẒAM ZARANDI, MOLLĀ MOḤAMMAD. E*ncyclopædia Iranica*, online edition, 2016, available at http://www.iranicaonline.org/articles/nabil-zarandi (accessed on 29 June 2019).

[53]"NABIL-E AʿẒAM ZARANDI, MOLLĀ MOḤAMMAD." *Encyclopædia Iranica*, online edition, 2016, available at http://www.iranicaonline.org/articles/nabil-zarandi (accessed on 29 June 2019).

[54]Nabíl-e Zarandi. *Masnavi-ye Nabíl-e Zarandi dar târikh-e amr-e Bahâ'i va so'ud-e Hazrat-e Bahâ Allâh. Cairo*: Mohyi al-Din Sabri-ye Kordi, 1924.

[55]Nabíl Zarandí. Mathnav*í-i-Nabíl-i-Zarandí.* Langenhain, Germany: Bahá'í Verlag, 1995.

[56]'Abdu'l-Bahá. *Memorials of the Faithful.* Wilmette, Bahá'í Publishing Trust, 1971,

inspiration, his poetic gift like a crystal stream". [57] 'Abdu'l-Bahá particularly referred to Nabíl's ode "Bahá, Bahá", which He states was written in a state of ecstasy. A few lines of this famous ode are reproduced below:

> Though the Night of Parting endless seem as thy nigh-black hair, Bahá, Bahá,
>
> Yet we meet at last, and the gloom is past in thy lightning's glare, Bahá, Bahá!
>
> To my heart from thee was a signal shown that I to all men should make known
>
> That they, as the ball to the goal doth fly, should to thee repair, Bahá, Bahá!
>
> At this my call from the quarters four men's hearts and souls to thy quarters pour:
>
> What, forsooth, could attract them more than that region fair, Bahá, Bahá?
>
> The World hath attained to Heaven's worth, and a Paradise is the face of earth
>
> Since at length thereon a breeze hath blown from thy nature rare, Bahá, Bahá!
>
> Bountiful art thou, as all men know: at a glance two worlds thou would'st e'en bestow
>
> On the suppliant hands of thy direst foe, if he makes his prayer, Bahá, Bahá![58]

Nabíl also wrote a poem describing the martyrdom of Hájí Mullá Hasan as follows:

> One of these was Hasan, an illuminating moon,
>
> whose hair had become like milk from following the path of loyalty.

---

p.33.

[57]'Abdu'l-Bahá. *Memorials of the Faithful.* Wilmette, Bahá'í Publishing Trust, 1971, p.35.

[58]E.G. Browne. *Materials for the Study of the Bábí Religion.* Cambridge, 1918, p.353.

He possessed piety and knowledge, yoked with resplendent deeds,

perseverance, and, in the face of calamity, the meekness of a lamb.

In a dream on that last night, his beloved Abhá appeared to him

like the illuminating sun and spoke to him these words:

"O Hasan," He said, "without any doubt your name has been entered

in the book of those who have offered up their lives for faith.

"But if you be not content with this fate,

tell me now that I may change your destiny."

"No, by God!" Hasan replied. "Would that I had a hundred souls

that I might gladly sacrifice them all at Your feet!"

The Monarch replied, "O true friend, since you are thus content,

your two fellow prisoners may be also blessed to share your destiny."

As soon as Hasan awakened from this dream,

he shared the promise with his companions.

They both said to him, "This is but vain imaginings!

It is certain that we all shall be freed tomorrow!"

"No, no!" Hasan replied. "Whether or not ye be content,

all three of us will be sacrificed this very day!

"The Beloved Himself has said so! There is no way

to countermand it! Be thou content with His desire!"

An hour had not passed ere from that place

all three were taken to the place of slaughter.

All three gave their lives away – Hasan with felicity,

the other two with great sighing and sorrow. [59]

Likewise, Nabíl composed a chronological poem of events in the life of Báhá'u'lláh. The poem was translated by Professor Edward Browne of the University of Cambridge and published in the 1889 issue[60] of the Journal of the Royal Asiatic Society of Great Britain and Ireland:

1. In the beginning of Ghirbál (= 1233 a.h.[61, 62] according to the abjad notation [63]) from the year of the Furkán (*i.e.* the Kur'an), on the second morning of Muharram, in Teherán, that King, who is the Creator of whomsoever is in the world (*lit.* in the Contingent World), turned His footsteps from the Unseen to the Visible (*lit.* Contingent) World.
2. After twice ten and seven (i.e. 27 years) of His pure life it was "sixty" (i.e. the year of the 'manifestation' of the Báb, a.h. 1260) [64], and there was mercy (shown) to the people of His land. He manifested His Supreme Name, so that creatures might comprehend him in that way.
3. At thirty-two (years) of age He started for the plain; the World became bright from the splendour of His visage; He met, to unfold His glories, with the form of Tá (probably Jenáb-i-Táhira, i.e. Kurratu'l-'Ayn) and Kuds (Jenáb-i-Kuddús, i.e. Hájí Mullá Muḥammad 'Ali Bálfúrushí) in the plain of Badasht.
4. At thirty-three He blossomed like a rose; that God of all set

[59]John S. Hatcher and Amrollah Hemmat. *Reunion with the Beloved: Poetry and Martyrdom.* Juxta Publishing Limited, Hong Kong, 2014, p. 82-83. Available online at: https://bahai-library.com/pdf/h/hatcher_hemmat_poetry_martyrdom.pdf

[60]Edward Granville Browne. The Bábís of Persia II – Their Literature and Doctrines. *The Journal of the Royal Asiatic Society of Great Britain and Ireland, vol.* 4, No. 4, 1889, pp. 881-1009.

[61]*a.h.* stands for *Anno Hegirae* or "in the year of the Hijra" which represents the beginning of the Islamic calendar.

[62]1233 a.h. is the year 1819 C.E. when Báhá'u'lláh was born.

[63]In the Abjad writing system each letter of Arabic calendar is assigned decimal numeral. Words therefore can have a numerical value when digits for each letter are added together.

[64]1260 a.h. is the year 1844 C.E. when the Báb declared His mission.

out for (the tomb of Sheykh) Tabarsí; on the way, by His own hidden Will, lie fell in with the people of tyranny at Amul.

5. At thirty-five that Monarch of dominion set out towards grief and calamity (there is a play on these words, Karb ú Belá and Karbalá). At thirty-six when He arrived at Teherán. He was imprisoned for four months with a hundred pains and griefs.
6. At thirty-seven the Monarch of Grace arrived at Baghdád with those of His household. At thirty-eight He disappeared from men, lifting up His standard like the Sun on the mountain-land.
7. At the age of forty He went from the plain to Zawrá (i.e. Baghdád); Zawrá in honour became like Yathrib and Baṭḥá? (i.e. Medina and Mecca); His lovers assembled from all directions (lit. from the four quarters); the standard of God (or 'of the truth') was set up by His rule.
8. At forty-seven that mighty Monarch came from 'írák (i.e. Baghdád) travelling to the Great City (i.e. Constantinople): for four months he was journeying like the bright sun with those of His household and His family and His companions.
9. At forty-eight that Giver of Purity to the earth became for four months a sojourner in the Great City (i.e. Constantinople): in the month of Rajab he reached the 'Land of the Mystery'; Edirne (Adrianople) became the envy of the highest Paradise.
10. When the age of that Wonderful Lord was fifty He tore from His face the veil; sparks fell into the soul of Paradise and the Devil (T*ághút*, which also signifies 'an idol'): the Sun of Behá [65] appeared from behind the cloud.
11. When His blessed age was fifty-three, His advance towards Jerusalem took place: in *Ghurfa* (this word, which is a name for the seventh, or highest heaven, stands in the abjad notation for 1285 [66], which is the year of the hijra intended), and on the twentieth of Rabí'uṣ-ṣání from Adrianople went forth the King of its glory.
12. On the twelfth day of Jamádi'ul-avval the King of nations (or

[65]The word *Behá* in this translation refers to Báhá'u'lláh.

[66]1285 a.h. is the year 1868 C.E. when Báhá'u'lláh was exiled to 'Akká.

creeds) arrived at Acre: it is settled that from beyond this strong prison all kingdoms will advance to His court.

13. It is now (the month of) Sha'bán of the year of Fúrú' (= 1286 a.h. [67]): the age of that King is fifty-four. It is now a full year and four months that this strong fortress (i.e. Acre) has been the abode of the Beloved.

14. This year the reckoning of the life of the Beloved is 'Life' (*ján* = 54, and means 'life,' or 'soul'): all the friends are lifeless through separation: the Beloved, who is this year established on the throne of 'Life' (*ján*) is ready to give life to those separated.

15. The King of Permanence with seventy people (i.e. followers) has made His abode in the most desolate of all cities (*i.e.* Acre): help Thine own religion (*amr*) Thyself, O King of Permanence; for Thee there is no other helper than Thyself.

16. How long shall Thy Branches (*aghsán*, 'branches,' is, as I have explained, the term applied to Behá's sons) be in the assembly of the enemy? How long shall Thy friends be scattered on every side? Give life to the troop of those separated from Thee: how long shall this people be lifeless?

17. Open this year the Gate of Meeting; give exaltation to the People of Behá this year; this year, when *ján* (soul, or life=54) is in conjunction with *furú'* (divisions, ramifications=1286) [68], exalt a standard from the Unseen this year.

18. O Nabíl, (make) a plan for thine own affairs; thou art forty years (old); make a change; ask for the cup of spiritual knowledge from God this year; how long wilt thou stick in the world of Words?

19. Thine age is forty, (yet) thou art nought but a fool; thou hast not entered in at the gate of the City of the Heart: they say that forty is the year of perfection: "thine age is forty, yet hast thou not become perfect."

---

[67] 1286 a.h is the year 1869 C.E. when Nabíl write this poem.

[68] 1286 *a.h* is the year 1869 C.E.

In this other poem, Nabíl extols the station of his Beloved One:[69]

Good news, O apparitions of holiness, for the Beauty of God is divulged !

O Zephyr ! convey to the quickened of heart a summons to his presence !

Ho ! ye peoples who expectantly await the Grace of the Mighty King,

The glorious Moon is publicly apparent, resplendent and beautiful.

The Apparition of the Eternal hath appeared to set up the standard of the Beyan ;

Exalted beyond the conception of worldlings fancy is the Most Holy Realm of Power.

That Signless King hath sat on the throne of majesty, and state ;

He hath thus greeted the sufferers of affliction : — 'O band who pretend to [my] love !

When anyone treads my path I will cry to him, that he may know,

That whosoever becomes enamoured of me shall not escape suffering and sorrow.

Should anyone not obey me, not take hold of the rope of my protection,

I will drive him far from my presence, I will give him in my wrath to the wind of Not (being).

I am Eternal : I am from the World of the Everlasting : I am One : I am from the Land of the Unlimited :

I am come after the children of the Spirit, and unto me do they advance.

Kindlings of the Fire of my Will ! Lo, am I not your Lord?

Pass to the place of the holy ones; hear the shrill cry of 'Yea!

[69]Edward G. Browne. Some remarks on the Babi texts edited by Baron Victor Rosen. The Journal of the Royal Asiatic Society, 1892, pp. 324-5.

> Yea!"
>
> I am that Manifestation of the All-Protecting! I am that Ark of Safety!
>
> I am that Impersonal Personality, and I have appeared in my Glory !
>
> I am the uplifted Tree of Life ! I am the Hidden and Apparent Fruit !
>
> I am the King of the Kings of the Beyan, and by me is the Beyan exalted !
>
> O witnesses of my fiery Apparition ! Hasten toward my country !
>
> Make your heads and lives my sacrifice ; for I am the Monarch of Kerbela !'

Without any doubt, in the future the believers will rise up to compile the fruitful literary work of Nabíl. He is certainly one of the first and foremost self-educated scholars of the Faith.

2. His indefatigable disciple

2.1 The Initial Contact.

Nabíl was born in the village of Zarand on 29 July 1831[70]. He came from a fairly simple family. He wrote about his childhood and family:

> My father belonged to the tribe of Táhirí, who led a nomadic life in the province of Khurásán. His name was Ghulám 'Alí, son of Ḥusayn-i-'Arab. He married the daughter of Kalb-'Alí, and by her had three sons and three daughters ... I was born on the eighteenth of Safar in the year 1247 A.H., in the village of Zarand. I was a shepherd by profession, and was given in my early days a most rudimentary education. I longed to devote more time to my studies, but was unable

[70]Vahid Rafati. NABIL-E A'ẒAM ZARANDI, MOLLĀ MOḤAMMAD. *Encyclopædia Iranica*, online edition, 2016, available at http://www.iranicaonline.org/articles/nabil-zarandi (accessed on 29 June 2019).

> to do so, owing to the exigencies of my situation. I read the Qur'án with eagerness, committed several of its passages to memory, and chanted them whilst I followed my flock over the fields. I loved solitude, and watched the stars at night with delight and wonder. In the quiet of the wilderness, I... supplicated the Almighty to guide my steps and enable me to find the Truth. My father oftentimes took me with him to Qum, where I became acquainted with the teachings of Islám and the ways and manners of its leaders. He was a devout follower of that Faith, and was closely associated with the ecclesiastical leaders who congregated in that city ...Gradually I came to perceive their insincerity and to loathe the baseness of their character. Eager as I was to ascertain the trustworthiness of the creeds and dogmas which they strove to impose upon me, I could neither find the time nor obtain the facilities with which to satisfy my desire. [71]

He was 16 years old when in 1847 he chanced upon the teachings while he was in a village. "Have you heard," said one of the two men, "that the Siyyid-i-Báb has been conducted to the village of Kinár-Gird and is on his way to Ṭihrán?" [72]

The ongoing conversation of these people fascinated young Nabíl's mind. He was instantly moved and eager to know more about the new Revelation. Such anxieties were turned to tranquility when a certain Siyyid Ḥusayn Zavarí'í passed through Zarand – Nabíl's native village—and informed him more fully of the meaning and nature of the Báb's Declaration.

This traveller, well-versed in the teachings of the new Faith, directed Nabíl to a cousin of his named Siyyid Ismá'íl who had attained the presence of Báb and who travelled to Qum every spring. Siyyid Ismá'íl was the first person to provide an in depth explanation of the teachings to Nabíl.

On that occasion Siyyid Ḥusayn showed Nabíl some of the writings

[71]Nabíl. *The Dawn-Breakers: Nabíl's Narrative of the Early Days of the Bahá'í Revelation.* US Bahá'í Publishing Trust, 1932, pp. 434.

[72]Nabíl. *The Dawn-Breakers: Nabíl's Narrative of the Early Days of the Bahá'í Revelation.* US Bahá'í Publishing Trust, 1932, pp. 435.

of the Báb. Reading these writings made a big impression on Nabíl's heart and encouraged him to make the trip to Qum. Nabíl managed to convince his father to allow him to go to Qum under the pretext of perfecting his knowledge of the Arabic language. While Persian was spoken in Iran, Arabic was considered the language of the educated.

Nabíl relates that a few days after arriving in Qum, his mother and sister arrived, to whom he taught the new Faith and who subsequently enrolled. He managed to meet Siyyid Ismá'íl who significantly extended Nabíl's knowledge of the Faith and who nurtured his thirst for understanding.

Enthused by his desire to render some service to the Cause, the young Nabíl asked Siyyid Ismá'íl what he should do. In response he was told about the ongoing episode in Ṭabarsí where a group of over 300 Bábís were being assailed in a precarious fort only because of their religious beliefs.

Nabíl immediately offered to help. However, Siyyid Ismá'íl recommended that he and another enthusiastic believer wait for a message that Siyyid Ismá'íl was planning to send from Ṭihrán. The long-awaited letter did not arrive and therefore Nabíl decided to travel to Ṭihrán. Upon arriving in Ṭihrán he found Siyyid Ismá'íl about to post the letter in the mail. Both Siyyid Ismá'íl and Nabíl began to make preparations to join the Bábís of Ṭabarsí. However, they then received news of the massacre of the brave defenders of Fort Ṭabarsí, causing profound consternation.

Soon after this Nabíl met his maternal uncle, who asked him to return to Zarand. Following the advice of Siyyid Ismá'íl, Nabíl left for his native village where he succeeded in converting his brother to the Faith. But Nabíl's heart was with his Bábí friends and he therefore managed to obtain his father's permission to return to the capital where he again met Siyyid Ismá'íl. Through him, Nabíl was introduced to an enlightened believer Mírzá Aḥmad who eventually became his beloved friend and tutor.

2.2 In Ṭihrán

Mírzá Aḥmad earned his living as a scribe and in his free time he dedicated himself to transcribing the Scriptures, making copies of the Bayán, the Báb's most prominent book. The association with such a soul represented for the young Nabíl a very valuable personal experience. Mírzá Aḥmad deepened Nabíl's knowledge of the teachings but more importantly, he served as a role model as a result of long periods of time together. In this way Nabíl received inspiration and encouragement for his future services to the Faith. I still feel", Nabíl wrote much later, "after the lapse of eight and thirty years since our first interview in Ṭihrán, the warmth of his friendship and the fervour of his faith."[73]

At times, Nabíl was in charge of taking the transcribed copies of the Writings as gifts to the friends of God. He especially remembered the time when he delivered those special presents to the wife of one of the combatants of Ṭabarsi.

Through Mírzá Aḥmad, Nabíl was introduced to the local community of believers with whom he closely associated for several months, making many new friends. The days of his sojourn in the capital were also characterized by his frequent visits to Bahá'u'lláh's home. He came to know the Blessed Beauty and shared precious time with the members of His family. Meeting 'Abdu'l-Bahá, then a young boy, was a treasured experience for Nabíl:

> On another occasion, when I visited that same house, I was on the point of entering the room that Mírzá Yaḥyá occupied, when Áqáy-i-Kalím, whom I had previously met, approached and requested me, since Iṣfandíyár, their servant, had gone to market and had not yet returned, to conduct "Áqá" to the Madrisiy-i-Mírzá-Ṣáliḥ in his stead and then return to this place. I gladly consented, and as I was preparing to leave, I saw the Most Great Branch, a child of exquisite beauty, wearing the kuláh [a hat] and cloaked in the jubbiy-i-hizari'í [a native coat], emerge from the room which His Father occupied, and descend the steps leading to the gate of the house. I advanced and stretched forth my arms to carry Him.
>
> "We shall walk together," He said, as He took hold of my

[73]Nabíl. *The Dawn-Breakers: Nabíl's Narrative of the Early Days of the Bahá'í Revelation.* US Bahá'í Publishing Trust, 1932, p. 169.

hand and led me out of the house. We chatted together as we walked hand in hand in the direction of the madrisih known in those days by the name of Pa-Minar. As we reached His classroom, He turned to me and said: "Come again this afternoon and take me back to my home, for Iṣfandíyár is unable to fetch me. My Father will need him to-day."

I gladly acquiesced, and returned immediately to the house of Bahá'u'lláh. There again I met Mírzá Yaḥyá, who delivered into my hands a letter which he asked me to take to the Madrisiy-i-Sadr and hand to Bahá'u'lláh, whom I was told I would find in the room occupied by Mullá Báqir-i-Bastamí. He asked me to bring back the reply immediately. I fulfilled the commission and returned to the madrisih in time to conduct the Most Great Branch to His home. " [74]

Nabíl also described in his immortal Narrative how the wife of Bahá'u'lláh cured him from an eye condition with an ointment prepared by herself. Through his engagement with the Holy Family, he realized the low nature of Mírzá Yaḥyá [75] and his incapacity in matters of the Faith. In addition, Nabíl interacted with Ḥájí Mírzá Siyyid 'Ali, the great uncle of the Báb who later became a martyr of the Cause, and glimpsed the lofty features of his character. It is also at this time that he met Vaḥíd, another extraordinary believer of the Báb, referred to as "the most learned, the most eloquent and influential" [76] among His disciples. Vaḥíd had learned about the Faith when he was sent as the Sháh's special emissary to investigate the new Faith. It was through association with these exemplary believers that Nabíl's devoted character was shaped.

This relatively peaceful atmosphere was brought to an end at the beginning of 1850 when the enemies of the Faith, comprising political and religious leaders, increased their hostility towards the Bábí community. The Ṭihrán Bábí community was suddenly the target of an

---

[74]Nabíl. *The Dawn-Breakers: Nabíl's Narrative of the Early Days of the Bahá'í Revelation.* US Bahá'í Publishing Trust, 1932, p. 441.

[75]Bahá'u'lláh's half-brother.

[76]Nabíl. *The Dawn-Breakers: Nabíl's Narrative of the Early Days of the Bahá'í Revelation.* US Bahá'í Publishing Trust, 1932, p. 171.

ordeal which reached its climax in the murder of seven Bábís, known as the Seven Martyrs of Tehran, all of whom were Nabíl's friends. Leading this systematic wave of persecutions was the city mayor.

This organized repression started when a treacherous individual delivered a list of names and addresses of the local believers to the authorities, facilitating the issuing of arrest orders. Eventually fourteen believers were arrested on the same day that Nabíl was in the capital being visited by his maternal uncle and brother from Zarand.

Out of the fourteen imprisoned believers, half of them retracted their faith under death threats. The remaining seven have been recorded in the history of the Cause of God as the Seven Martyrs of Ṭihrán, killed publicly and savagely by beheading in February 1850.

When Nabíl returned to the place where he was staying, he found a message from Mírzá Aḥmad in his room. The note made him aware of the danger of the moment and urged him to join him in the Madrisih Sháh where he would be safe.

In the meantime, Bahá'u'lláh sent a letter to Mírzá Aḥmad informing him of the sinister purposes of the Prime Minister who was attempting to hurt the community. In the communication, Mírzá Aḥmad was asked to leave the city and instruct his disciple — the young Nabíl — to return to Zarand.

The news from the capital created concern amongst Nabíl's relatives about his fate. His father heard erroneously that Nabíl had been arrested and was about to be executed. His relatives hurried to the capital and asked him to return with them. Thus Nabíl said goodbye to Mírzá Aḥmad and returned to his home, arriving to his home at the time of the national holiday, Naw-Rúz (New Year).

The young man's arrival was happily celebrated by his family and he was surrounded by the greatest care within his home. But Nabíl's mind and heart were occupied with the threat to his beloved Ṭihráni friends. He wrote in his *Narrative:*

> In the midst of the festivities which my relatives celebrated in Zarand, my heart was set upon Ṭihrán, and my thoughts centred round the fate which might have befallen my fellow-disciples in that agitated city. I longed to hear of their safety.

> Though in the house of my father, and surrounded with the solicitude of my parents, I felt oppressed by the thought of being severed from that little band, whose perils I could well imagine and whose afflictions I longed to share.
>
> The terrible suspense under which I lived, while confined in my home, was unexpectedly relieved by the arrival of Ṣádiq-i-Tabrízí, who came from Ṭihrán and was received in the house of my father. Though delivering me from the uncertainties which had been weighing so heavily upon me, he, to my profound horror, unfolded to my ears a tale of such terrifying cruelty that the anxieties of suspense paled before the ghastly light which that lurid story cast upon my heart."[77]

Shortly after this, the repression intensified throughout the country, and the blessed Báb was executed in the central square of Tabríz on 9 July 1850.

2.3 In 'Iráq, Kirmánsháh and Baghdád

Nabíl harbored the desire to meet Mírzá Aḥmad again, who was, at this time (unbeknownst to Nabíl) residing in Ṭihrán. Such sentiments led him to leave Zarand for Qum, but Nabíl did not find him there. He received information that he would find him in the city of Káshán, wherefore he left for that place, but returned disappointed.

Returning to Qum, he was informed by a certain friend associated with his dear tutor that he had recently accompanied Mírzá Aḥmad to the town of Kirmánsháh. Through contacts, Nabíl was guided to the neighbouring city of Hamadan where he was given an address and the assurance that this person would receive him and lead him to the presence of Mírzá Aḥmad. This is how it happened:

> A few days after my arrival, Mírzá Aḥmad informed me of his having succeeded, while in Qum, in teaching the Cause to Íldírím Mírzá, brother of Khánlar Mírzá, to whom he wished to present a copy of the "Dalá'il-i-Sab'ih," and expressed his desire that I should be its bearer. Íldírím Mírzá was in those

[77]Nabíl. *The Dawn-Breakers: Nabíl's Narrative of the Early Days of the Bahá'í Revelation*. US Bahá'í Publishing Trust, 1932, p. 445.

days governor of K͟hurram-Ábád, in the province of Luristán, and had encamped with his army in the mountains of K͟havih-Valis͟htar. I was only too glad to grant his request, and expressed my readiness to start immediately on that journey. With a Kurdish guide, we traversed mountains and forests for six days and six nights, until we reached the governor's headquarters. I delivered the trust into his hands and brought back with me for Mírzá Aḥmad a written message from him expressing his appreciation of the gift and assuring him of his devotion to the Cause of its Author.

On my return, I received from Mírzá Aḥmad the joyful tidings of the arrival of Bahá'u'lláh in Kirmáns͟háh. As we were being ushered into His presence, we found Him, it being the month of Ramadán, engaged in reading the Qur'án, and were blessed by hearing Him read verses of that sacred Book. I presented to Him Íldírím Mírzá's written message to Mírzá Aḥmad. "The faith which a member of the Qájár dynasty professes," He remarked, after reading the letter, "cannot be depended upon. His declarations are insincere. Expecting that the Bábís will one day assassinate the sovereign, he harbours in his heart the hope of being acclaimed by them the successor. The love he professes for the Báb is actuated by that motive." Within a few months we knew the truth of His words. This same Íldírím Mírzá gave orders that a certain Siyyid Basir-i-Hindí, a fervent adherent of the Faith, should be put to death.[78]

Bahá'u'lláh stayed in the city of Kirmáns͟háh for about a month around August 1851 before leaving for Karbilá. Then, He called Nabíl and Mírzá Aḥmad to His presence and expressed His wish that they return to Ṭihrán. Nabíl, particularly, was commissioned to take Mírzá Yaḥyá to a certain place in the capital until He Himself returned there. Nabíl wrote about Mírzá Yaḥyá's disobedience:

> Mírzá Yaḥyá, to whom I delivered the message, refused to leave Ṭihrán, and directed me instead to leave for Qazvín. He compelled me to abide by his wish and to take with

---

[78]Nabíl. *The Dawn-Breakers: Nabíl's Narrative of the Early Days of the Bahá'í Revelation.* US Bahá'í Publishing Trust, 1932, pp. 587-588.

me certain letters which he bade me deliver to certain of his friends in that town. On my return to Ṭihrán, I was constrained, on the insistence of my kinsmen, to leave for Zarand. Mírzá Aḥmad, however, promised that he would again arrange for my return to the capital, a promise which he fulfilled. Two months later, I was again living with him in a caravanserai outside the gate of Naw, where I passed the whole winter in his company.

He spent his days in transcribing the Persian Bayán and the "Dalá'il-i-Sab'ih,"[79] a work he accomplished with admirable enthusiasm. He entrusted me with two copies of the latter, asking me to present them on his behalf to Mustawfiyu'l-Mamalik-i-Ashtiyání and Mírzá Siyyid 'Alíy-i-Tafarshí, surnamed the Majdu'l-Ashraf. The former was so much affected that he was completely won over to the Faith. As for Mírzá Siyyid 'Alí, the views he expressed were of a totally different character. At a gathering at which Áqáy-i-Kalím[80] was present, he commented in an unfavourable manner upon the continued activities of the believers.

"This sect," he publicly declared, "is still living. Its emissaries are hard at work, spreading the teachings of their leader. One of them, a youth, came to visit me the other day, and presented me with a treatise which I regard as highly dangerous. Anyone from among the common people who shall read that book will surely be beguiled by its tone." Áqáy-i-Kalím immediately understood from his allusions that Mírzá Aḥmad had sent the Book to him and that I had acted as his messenger. On that very day, Áqáy-i-Kalím asked me to visit him and advised me to return to my home in Zarand.

I was asked to induce Mírzá Aḥmad to leave instantly for Qum, as both of us, in his opinion, were exposed to great danger. Acting according to Mírzá Aḥmad's instructions, I succeeded in inducing the siyyid to return the Book that had

---

[79] The "Dalá'il-i-Sab'ih" (The Seven Proofs) was a book revealed by the Báb' in the fortress of Máh-Kú

[80] Bahá'u'lláh's brother.

been offered him. Shortly after, I parted company with Mírzá Aḥmad, whom I never met again. I accompanied him as far as Sháh-'Abdu'l-'Azim, while he departed for Qum, while I pursued my way to Zarand.[81]

2.4 After the Martyrdom of the Báb

Following the martyrdom of the Báb in July 1850 Nabíl began intensely promoting the new Revelation. He served a prison term in Sáva for four months because of his teaching activities. He was also engaged in transcribing and circulating the writings of the Báb,[82]

After the martyrdom of the Báb in 1850, the community of His followers fell into a state of lethargy and inaction. By then, many of its leading figures had disappeared and the good name of the congregation was tainted by the irresponsibility and misconduct of some of its publicly known members including Mírzá Yaḥyá.

Bahá'u'lláh had been imprisoned in the most dirty and horrible prison in the capital before being banished to Baghdád in August 1853 where he was living. He had been stripped of his earthly possessions and all of his property had been confiscated.

Even in this state of affairs the Bábís remained attentive to the promises that the Báb had left them about the imminent appearance of a greater Messenger of God, for whom He had come to prepare the way. In a vast portion of his writings, the Báb explained that "He whom God will make manifest" would appear publicly before the eyes of men in the course of the year 1863.

In the period following the Báb's martyrdom in 1850, there were several people who dared to claim such a station. Nabíl, contemplating the low condition in which the Bábí community had fallen from a reputation earned with the blood of thousands of martyrs was among them that made certain claims, attributing to himself the position of the promised Messenger. Other believers made similar claims. Many of these, including Nabíl, ended up repenting sincerely at the feet of

---

[81]Nabíl. *The Dawn-Breakers: Nabíl's Narrative of the Early Days of the Bahá'í Revelation*. US Bahá'í Publishing Trust, 1932, p. 592.

[82]Vahid Rafati. NABIL-E A'ẒAM ZARANDI, MOLLĀ MOḤAMMAD. E*ncyclopædia Iranica*, online edition, 2016, available at http://www.iranicaonline.org/articles/nabil-zarandi (accessed on 29 June 2019).

Bahá'u'lláh in Baghdád.

This strong decline of the Bábís caused Bahá'u'lláh to leave the city and retire to a solitary life in the mountains of Sulaymáníyyih for two years. In the Kitáb-i-Iqán, He describes those days in this way:

> In the early days of Our arrival in this land, when We discerned the signs of impending events, We decided, ere they happened, to retire. We betook Ourselves to the wilderness, and there, separated and alone, led for two years a life of complete solitude. From Our eyes there rained tears of anguish, and in Our bleeding heart there surged an ocean of agonizing pain. Many a night We had no food for sustenance, and many a day Our body found no rest. By Him Who hath My being between His hands! notwithstanding these showers of afflictions and unceasing calamities, Our soul was wrapt in blissful joy, and Our whole being evinced an ineffable gladness. [83]

Nabíl observed with disappointment the state into which the Bábí community had fallen.

The Guardian of the Faith wrote:

> Nabíl, traveling at that time through the province of Khurásán, the scene of the tumultuous early victories of a rising Faith, had himself summed up his impressions of the prevailing condition. "The fire of the Cause of God," he testifies in his narrative, "had been well-nigh quenched in every place. I could detect no trace of warmth anywhere." In Qazvín, according to the same testimony, the remnant of the community had split into four factions, bitterly opposed to one another, and a prey to the most absurd doctrines and fancies. [84]
>
> As the character of the professed adherents of the Báb declined and as proofs of the deepening confusion that afflicted them multiplied, the mischief-makers, who were lying in wait, and whose sole aim was to exploit the

[83]Bahá'u'lláh. *The Kitáb-i-Íqán.* US Bahá'í Publishing Trust, 1989, p. 250.

[84]Shoghi Effendi. *God Passes By.* US Bahá'í Publishing Trust, 1979, p.113.

> progressive deterioration in the situation for their own benefit, grew ever more and more audacious. The conduct of Mírzá Yaḥyá, who claimed to be the successor of the Báb, and who prided himself on his high sounding titles of Mir'átu'l-Azalíyyih (Everlasting Mirror), of Ṣubḥ-i-Azal (Morning of Eternity), and of Ismu'l-Azal (Name of Eternity), and particularly the machinations of Siyyid Muḥammad[85], exalted by him to the rank of the first among the "Witnesses" of the Bayán, were by now assuming such a character that the prestige of the Faith was becoming directly involved, and its future security seriously imperiled.[86]

In September 1854 Nabíl set out for Baghdád to turn to Bahá'u'lláh, his old acquaintance and counselor in Tehran. He was desperately seeking a firm pillar, immune from the evils that were afflicting the Bábí community. Alas, Bahá'u'lláh had withdrawn to the mountains for two years and His whereabouts were not known, while the only known Bábí figure was Mírzá Yaḥyá, Bahá'u'lláh's half-brother.

Despite having noticed Mírzá Yaḥyá's insincerity and lack of courage in Tehran, Nabíl proposed to meet him again. The frank and moving way in which Nabíl approached the search for "He Whom God Will Make Manifest", allows us to appreciate his resolute character, his unwavering will and above all his deep devotion to the Faith of the Báb.

Let Ḥasan Balyuzi give us an enlightening account of what Nabíl had to go through before taking refuge under the shadow of Bahá'u'lláh's infallible protection.

> Mullá Muḥammad-i-Zarandí, later entitled Nabíl-i-A'zam, destined to become the most outstanding chronicler and historian of the Bábí-Bahá'í Faith, and who had himself made certain claims, reached Baghdád at a time when Bahá'u'lláh was at Sulaymáníyyih. By his own admission, he still believed that Mírzá Yaḥyá was a man of consequence and sought a

[85]Mírzá Yaḥyá's close associate.

[86]Shoghi Effendi. *God Passes By.* US Bahá'í Publishing Trust, 1979, p.114.

meeting with him. Mírzá Músá, Áqáy-i-Kalím [87], whom Nabíl encountered on the bridge, took him home (to the house of 'Alí Madad) to meet the Most Great Branch, then barely ten years old. From Mírzá Músá he learned that Mírzá Yaḥyá did not meet anyone, and so it was, for not only did Mírzá Yaḥyá not show his face, but he sent Nabíl a message, urging him to quit Baghdád and seek the safety of Karbilá where Siyyid Muḥammad-i-Isfahání had stationed himself.

In Karbilá, Nabíl carefully watched Siyyid Muḥammad's riotous behaviour and childish pranks, and eventually recorded them. He was unhappy. He had dared to claim leadership; he had not found in Mírzá Yaḥyá a 'shepherd' of a battered and mutilated flock. He writes very movingly of his spiritual odyssey — of Bahá'u'lláh's return from Sulaymáníyyih [in March 1856], attainment to His presence, finding in Him all that he desired, doing penance at His door, coming upon Áqá Muḥammad-Ibrahím-i-Amír-i-Nayrízí sweeping the roadway and taking the broom from him to do likewise (the act of a humble penitent), performing a ceremonial ablution in the Tigris (symbolic of washing away all the stains of the past), divesting himself of the robes of a would-be priest. With his rebirth, Nabíl composed a translucent poem, which Bahá'u'lláh lovingly and graciously acknowledged, assuring Nabíl that that poem had set the seal on and completely redeemed the past. Now, at long last, Mullá Muḥammad-i-Zarandí [Nabíl] was at peace with himself and with the world. When Bahá'u'lláh was told that Mullá Muḥammad [Nabíl], whom He eventually honoured with the designation of Nabíl-i-A'ẓam, had been sweeping the roadway outside His house, He administered a gentle reproof to His attendant for having allowed it, and said, 'This makes Me feel ashamed', which, when Nabíl heard of it, brought to his mind the famous lines of the poet Sa'dí (the reflection of a verse in the Qur'án):

'Consider the generosity and the kindliness of the Lord

[87]Bahá'u'lláh's brother and loyal believer.

Sinned the servant has, but ashamed is He.' [88]

As a sign of his own humiliation, he also cut off his beard.

Nabíl remained for three months in Baghdád, after which, in October 1856, Bahá'u'lláh sent him to Qazvin, Persia, to teach the Faith.[89] He also visited his native Zarand, Hamadan and other major Bábí congregations. The trip was paid for by the Blessed Beauty. Initially Nabíl did not want to accept the money that was passed to him by a believer at the city gate. However, as the believer insisted, Nabíl ultimately gratefully accepted this support from Bahá'u'lláh.

The experiences of that trip were indelibly engraved in his mind: "Every instant a new door would fling open before me. It was as if I had wings to soar in the Heaven of the Beloved. I felt no need to have a companion on the road and I had no fear of highwaymen."[90]

2.5 "Oh for the joy of those days ..."

On his return to Baghdád twenty months later in July 1858, Nabíl was instructed by Bahá'u'lláh to verify the fidelity of a copy of a writing from the Báb on which Siyyid Isma'il — one of Nabíl's first teachers - was working. Nabíl recorded that the job took eighteen days. Siyyid Ismá'il died shortly afterwards as a sacrifice on the path of the Cause and was called by Bahá'u'lláh the 'Beloved and Pride of the Martyrs'.

The unpublished chronicles of Nabíl cover this entire period. It describes how Nabíl shared a house with some other believers at a location close to a place visited continuously by the Blessed Beauty. Also, acting according to His advice, all the friends, among them Nabíl, took Turkish nationality for themselves, so that they could henceforth receive the protection of the Turkish government authorities.

The atmosphere that surrounded the meetings of the Bábí friends,

[88] Hasan Balyuzi. *Bahá'u'lláh, the King of Glory.* George Ronald Oxford, 1991, pp. 128-129.

[89] Vahid Rafati. NABIL-E A'ẒAM ZARANDI, MOLLĀ MOḤAMMAD. *Encyclopædia Iranica*, online edition, 2016, available at http://www.iranicaonline.org/articles/nabil-zarandi (accessed on 29 June 2019).

[90] Hasan Balyuzi. *Bahá'u'lláh, the King of Glory.* George Ronald Oxford, 1991, pp. 131-132.

their great love for Bahá'u'lláh and the extraordinary empowerment that He managed to instill in their hearts, is captured in the following words of Nabíl, who wrote:

> So inebriated, so carried away was every one by the sweet savors of the Morn of Divine Revelation that, methinks, out of every thorn sprang forth heaps of blossoms, and every seed yielded innumerable harvests.[91]
>
> The room of the Most Great House set apart for the reception of Bahá'u'lláh's visitors, though dilapidated, and having long since outgrown its usefulness, vied, through having been trodden by the blessed footsteps of the Well Beloved, with the Most Exalted Paradise. Low-roofed, it yet seemed to reach to the stars, and though it boasted but a single couch, fashioned from the branches of palms, whereon He Who is the King of Names was wont to sit, it drew to itself, even as a loadstone, the hearts of the princes.[92]
>
> So intoxicated were those who had quaffed from the cup of Bahá'u'lláh's presence, that in their eyes the palaces of kings appeared more ephemeral than a spider's web. The celebrations and festivities that were theirs were such as the kings of the earth had never dreamt of. I [Nabíl] myself with two others lived in a room which was devoid of furniture. Bahá'u'lláh entered it one day, and, looking about Him, remarked: 'Its emptiness pleases Me. In My estimation it is preferable to many a spacious palace, inasmuch as the beloved of God are occupied in it with the remembrance of the Incomparable Friend, with hearts that are wholly emptied of the dross of this world.'[93]

According to Shoghi Effendi, Bahá'u'lláh's "life was characterized by that same austerity, and evinced that same simplicity which

[91]Adapted from: Shoghi Effendi. *God Passes By.* US Bahá'í Publishing Trust, 1979, p.134

[92]Adapted from: Shoghi Effendi. *God Passes By.* US Bahá'í Publishing Trust, 1979, p.134

[93]Adapted from: Shoghi Effendi. *God Passes By.* US Bahá'í Publishing Trust, 1979, p.137.

marked the lives of His beloved companions. There was a time in 'Iráq He Himself affirms in one of His Tablets, "when the Ancient Beauty ... had no change of linen. The one shirt He possessed would be washed, dried and worn again." [94] According to Nabíl

> Many a night, no less than ten persons subsisted on no more than a pennyworth of dates. No one knew to whom actually belonged the shoes, the cloaks, or the robes that were to be found in their houses. Whoever went to the bazaar could claim that the shoes upon his feet were his own, and each one who entered the presence of Bahá'u'lláh could affirm that the cloak and robe he then wore belonged to him. Their own names they had forgotten, their hearts were emptied of aught else except adoration for their Beloved.... O, for the joy of those days, and the gladness and wonder of those hours! [95]
>
> Many a night would Mírzá Áqá Ján[96] gather them together in his room, close the door, light numerous camphorated candles, and chant aloud to them the newly revealed odes and Tablets in his possession. Wholly oblivious of this contingent world, completely immersed in the realms of the spirit, forgetful of the necessity for food, sleep or drink, they would suddenly discover that night had become day, and that the sun was approaching its zenith. [97]

That spiritual rejoicing, however, had its end for it was interrupted when the royal decree of the Sultan of Turkey came calling Bahá'u'lláh, His family and a group of believers, to the capital city of Constantinople and seat of government. Although disguised as an invitation, it was a forced exile promoted by His opponents.

Before departing, Bahá'u'lláh withdrew with His disciples for twelve days to the garden of Najíbíyyih, on the outskirts of

[94]Shoghi Effendi. *God Passes By.* US Bahá'í Publishing Trust, 1979, p.137.

[95]Adapted from: Shoghi Effendi. *God Passes By.* US Bahá'í Publishing Trust, 1979, p.137.

[96]Bahá'u'lláh's amanuensis.

[97]Adapted from: Shoghi Effendi. *God Passes By.* US Bahá'í Publishing Trust, 1979, p.152.

Baghdád. Bahá'u'lláh renamed this place the Garden of Riḍván (The Garden of Paradise). This green space was the setting for the Declaration to His family and a handful of Bábís that He was the Greatest Manifestation, predicted by the Báb and by all the Messengers of the past. The announcement filled the hearts of the believers with joy, and their spirits were high.

Three of those twelve memorable days have been designated Holy Days. The first day commemorates the day when Bahá'u'lláh crossed the riverbank to the garden with His entourage. This took place on 21 April 1863 at approximately three o'clock in the afternoon. The second is the ninth day, when the members of His family enter the garden. The third was the last day of the twelve day period, when the long trip to Constantinople began.

Nabíl, present during the period of the Declaration of Bahá'u'lláh, recalled with his pen those days what happened inside the Garden of Paradise. His record constitutes one the few eyewitness descriptions of this momentous occasion:

> Every day, ere the hour of dawn, the gardeners would pick the roses which lined the four avenues of the garden, and would pile them in the center of the floor of His blessed tent. So great would be the heap that when His companions gathered to drink their morning tea in His presence, they would be unable to see each other across it. All these roses Bahá'u'lláh would, with His own hands, entrust to those whom He dismissed from His presence every morning to be delivered, on His behalf, to His Arab and Persian friends in the city.
>
> One night, the ninth night of the waxing moon, I happened to be one of those who watched beside His blessed tent. As the hour of midnight approached, I saw Him issue from His tent, pass by the places where some of His companions were sleeping, and begin to pace up and down the moonlit, flower-bordered avenues of the garden. So loud was the singing of the nightingales on every side that only those who were near Him could hear distinctly His voice. He continued to walk until, pausing in the midst of one of these avenues, He observed: 'Consider these nightingales. So great is their

> love for these roses, that sleepless from dusk till dawn, they warble their melodies and commune with burning passion with the object of their adoration. How then can those who claim to be afire with the rose-like beauty of the Beloved choose to sleep?' For three successive nights I watched and circled round His blessed tent. Every time I passed by the couch whereon He lay, I would find Him wakeful, and every day, from morn till eventide, I would see Him ceaselessly engaged in conversing with the stream of visitors who kept flowing in from Baghdád. Not once could I discover in the words He spoke any trace of dissimulation." [98]

Bahá'u'lláh left the Garden on May 3, 1863. Although the name of Nabíl had not been included in the list of the twenty believers who should accompany Bahá'u'lláh to Constantinople, wearing a Dervish dress he later joined the entourage enthusiastically at the place called Ma'dán-Mis. They arrived Constantinople, (formerly Byzantium and today Istanbul), on August 16, 1863 after three and a half months.

2.6 Missions in Constantinople and Adrianople

Nabíl was in the company of Bahá'u'lláh for the three and a half month period of His sojourn in Constantinople. This stay ended when the Sultan of Turkey issued another edict ordering a further exile of the Blessed Beauty to the city of Adrianople, 250 kilometers away.

It was evident that the adversaries of the Faith had petitioned the royal court for this further exile to take place. The Turkish authorities decided to choose a city where the influence of the Cause was relatively insignificant. They decided on Adrianople, a rather old city, mostly inhabited by Christian people, whom, they thought, would not be receptive to the teachings of the Faith. Bahá'u'lláh called Adrianople the Remote Prison.

Before the departure, the believers were dismissed from the city by Bahá'u'lláh, except for a few who would continue the journey. They were given money to cover the expenses of the trip and Nabíl particularly, the night before the departure, was entrusted with the

[98]Adapted from: Shoghi Effendi. *God Passes By.* US Bahá'í Publishing Trust, 1979, p. 153

mission of going to Persia. 'Abdu'l-Bahá pointed out: "In Constantinople he was directed to return to Persia and there teach the Cause of God; also to travel throughout the country, and acquaint the believers in its cities and villages with all that had taken place". [99]

As Vahid Rafati has noted, three of Nabíl's major contributions were that as part of "his early travels as a Bahá'í, he met with the Bábí communities to invite them to the Bahá'í faith; he attracted the Bábi leaders to the recognition of Bahá'u'lláh as the fulfillment of the Báb's prophecies concerning the promised messianic figure and helped reinforce the belief of the new Bahá'ís in the teachings and principles that were being advanced by Bahá'u'lláh."[100]

Although Nabíl did not go directly to Adrianople, he wrote in his Narrative of the harsh conditions of the journey to Adrianople which had been endured by Bahá'u'lláh:

> A banishment endured with such meekness that the pen sheddeth tears when recounting it, and the page is ashamed to bear its description ... A cold of such intensity prevailed that year, that nonagenarians could not recall its like. In some regions, in both Turkey and Persia, animals succumbed to its severity and perished in the snows. The upper reaches of the Euphrates, in Ma'dan-Nuqrih, were covered with ice for several days—an unprecedented phenomenon—while in Díyár-Bakr the river froze over for no less than forty days. [101]

To obtain water from the springs," one of the companions recalled, "a great fire had to be lighted in their immediate neighborhood, and kept burning for a couple of hours before they thawed out."[102]

If Constantinople was the scene for Bahá'u'lláh's Declaration of

---

[99]'Abdu'l-Bahá. *Memorials of the Faithful.* Wilmette, Bahá'í Publishing Trust, 1971, p.33.

[100]Vahid Rafati. NABIL-E A'ẒAM ZARANDI, MOLLĀ MOḤAMMAD. E*ncyclopædia Iranica*, online edition, 2016, available at http://www.iranicaonline.org/articles/nabil-zarandi (accessed on 29 June 2019).

[101]Adapted from: Shoghi Effendi. *God Passes By.* US Bahá'í Publishing Trust, 1979, p. 161.

[102]Adapted from: Shoghi Effendi. Go*d Passes By.* US Bahá'í Publishing Trust, 1979, p. 161.

His Mission to a limited audience, Adrianople was the space for the open Proclamation of His Mission to the world. There the Prisoner of two empires sent epistles to the "crowned heads" of the time and summoned them to recognize the Sun of Divine Revelation.

According to Moojan Momen

> During this journey, in early 1866, Bahá'u'lláh wrote to him in Tehran, announcing to him his claim and instructing Zarandí to proclaim this openly. Zarandí then took the claim of Bahá'u'lláh to other Bábi communities, going from Tehran to travel throughout Khurásán (spring 1866) and then on to Yazd, Iṣfahán, Shíráz (autumn 1866), Tehran, Hamadán, Kirmánsháh and Baghdád (March 1867). During the course of this journey, at Na'ín, he met Mírzá Ja'far Yazdí, who informed him that Bahá'u'lláh had given the title Nabíl A'zam and instructed him to be the first person to carry out the ritual Bahá'í pilgrimage to both the House of the Báb and the House of Bahá'u'lláh in Baghdád. He then went on to Edirne to meet Bahá'u'lláh ...
>
> An indication of his fearlessness is that in one occasion in Bushrúyih in the early summer of 1866, when he knew that a mob of criminal elements of the town had been commissioned by a *muhtajid* to attack him, he nevertheless dispersed a group of Bahá'ís who had gathered to protect him and instructed his companion to leave the door of their house unlocked at night to demonstrate that these opponents were not worthy of consideration. On another occasion, in January 1867, when officials were searching for him throughout Tehran, he boldly went to the Anbar prison in order to visit a Bahá'í Riḍá-Qulí Khán Afshar, who was imprisoned there"[103]

'Abdu'l-Bahá commented on Nabíl's successful activities in the field of teaching in Persia after returning from Constantinople and Adrianople:

[103]Moojan Momen. *The Bahá'í Communities of Iran*. George Ronald Oxford, 2015, pp. 108-109.

> When this mission was accomplished, and the drums of "Am I not your Lord?" were rolling out—for it was the "year eighty"[104] —Nabíl hurried to Adrianople, crying as he went, "Yea verily Thou art! Yea verily!" and "Lord, Lord, here am I!" He entered Bahá'u'lláh's presence and drank of the red wine of allegiance and homage. [105]

According to Shoghi Effendi

> It was during those days that Nabíl, recently honored with the title of Nabíl-i-A'zam, in a Tablet specifically addressed to him, in which he was bidden to "deliver the Message" of his Lord "to East and West," arose, despite intermittent persecutions, to tear asunder the "most grievous veil," to implant the love of an adored Master in the hearts of His countrymen, and to champion the Cause which his Beloved had, under such tragic conditions, proclaimed. It was during those same days that Bahá'u'lláh instructed this same Nabíl to recite on His behalf the two newly revealed Tablets of the Pilgrimage, and to perform, in His stead, the rites prescribed in them, when visiting the Báb's House in Shíráz and the Most Great House in Baghdád—an act that marks the inception of one of the holiest observances, which, in a later period, the Kitáb-i-Aqdas was to formally establish. [106]

In this Most Holy Book these two Houses are designated as the most valuable places on earth in the eyes of God. It is prescribed as an obligation for all faithful to observe the pilgrimage to these two Houses that were blessed by the presence of the two Twin Manifestations.

Nabíl fulfilled with utmost devotion the performance of the rites. The ceremony specific to the House of the Báb begins from outside the city and continues along the path that leads to the House and then within the House. It is said that when people saw Nabíl through the streets wholly absorbed in the fulfillment of the extensive

[104]A reference to Bahá'u'lláh's declaration of His Mission in 1863, as the Báb's Promised One.

[105]'Abdu'l-Bahá. *Memorials of the Faithful.* Wilmette, Bahá'í Publishing Trust, 1971, pp. 33-34.

[106]Shoghi Effendi. *God Passes By.* US Bahá'í Publishing Trust, 1979, p. 176-177.

rite, they thought that he may have lost his mind. The two Tablets of the pilgrimage are called Súriy-i-Ḥajj, I and II.

> Soon after His Declaration near Baghdád, Bahá'u'lláh sent Nabíl-i-A'zam to Persia to announce the momentous news to the Bábís. Nabíl went to the home of Áqá Mírzá Áqá, and announced the joyful tidings to the believers in Shíráz. Áqá Mírzá Áqá immediately gave his allegiance to Bahá'u'lláh and considered himself a humble servant at His threshold. On one occasion the wife of the Báb, who was seated behind a curtain, heard Nabíl inform the friends that the Blessed Beauty was the Promised One of the Bayán, 'Him Whom God shall make Manifest'. No sooner did that noble woman hear this announcement than she put her forehead to the ground in adoration of her newly-found Lord and is reported to have whispered to her nephew: 'offer at His sacred threshold my most humble devotion.' Thus the bonds of love and adoration which had united these two became strengthened through their immediate response to the Cause they had both spontaneously espoused.[107]

On that occasion, Nabíl also brought gifts for the wife of the Báb. She immediately accepted the message brought by Nabíl that Bahá'u'lláh was the Promised One referred to by the Báb:

'Abdu'l-Bahá has referred to Nabíl's tirelessness as a traveling teacher of the Faith:

> He was then given specific orders to travel everywhere, and in every region to raise the call that God was now made manifest: to spread the blissful tidings that the Sun of Truth had risen. He was truly on fire, driven by restive love. With great fervor he would pass through a country, bringing this best of all messages and reviving the hearts. He flamed like a torch in every company, he was the star of every assemblage, to all who came he held out the intoxicating cup. [108]

---

[107]Adib Taherzadeh. *The Revelation of Bahá'u'lláh,* vol 4. George Ronald Oxford, 1974, p. 329.

[108]Abdu'l-Bahá. *Memorials of the Faithful.* Wilmette, Bahá'í Publishing Trust, 1971, p.34.

Nabíl's trip to Baghdád and Shíráz extended to other places including the province of Khurásán and the capital where he stayed for four months from November 1865 to clarify Mírzá Yaḥyá's claims.[109] In the village of Níshápúr he met Badí, then a rebellious young man with no interest in the teachings of the Faith, despite the fact that his father was a devoted and faithful believer. Nabíl related that he called the young man to his presence and shared with him passages from a very touching ode written by the Blessed Perfection, in which he describes His tribulations in the mountains of Sulaymáníyyih. The reading of those verses produced an instant and miraculous transformation in the behavior and attitude of Badí. The young man immediately embraced the Faith and years later was martyred for serving as an emissary of Bahá'u'lláh to the Sháh of Iran.

2.7 An Important Mission in Egypt

When, in Adrianople, Mírzá Yaḥyá openly manifested his malice against Bahá'u'lláh, Nabíl was the bearer of a Tablet revealed by the Supreme Pen in which Mírzá Yaḥyá was summoned to clarify his claims in a public way. Mírzá Yaḥyá, was at that time challenging the authority of Bahá'u'lláh and attributing Baha'u'llah's station to himself.

As a consequence of this rebellion, Bahá'u'lláh broke off all contact and relationship with this impostor and moved His residence to another place. Just prior to this He revealed the Súriy-i-Damm (Sura of the Blood), in honor of Nabíl.

Nabíl was the privileged recipient of delicate and far-reaching missions in the name of the Manifestation of God. On one occasion, Nabíl was sent to Turkey with the instruction to bring the brother of Bahá'u'lláh - Aqáy-i-Kalím - to Adrianople. This faithful brother of Bahá'u'lláh had travelled to Turkey in order to inform a believer named Mír Muḥammad of the outrageous claims made by Mírzá Yaḥyá.

Upon his return from Persia, Nabíl was once again entrusted with an important mission. It pertained to Mírzá Ḥaydar-'Alí, a prominent Bahá'í teacher, who while teaching the Faith in Egypt, was arbitrarily detained by the authorities, banished and imprisoned in the Sudan.

[109]Moojan Momen. *The Bahá'í Communities of Iran.* George Ronald Oxford, 2015.

Bahá'u'lláh commissioned Nabíl to address the Khedive of Egypt[110] and appeal to him to release this believer and six others in similar situations. Nabíl undertook the trip to Cairo. While walking through the streets of that city, he was discovered by elements of the Persian Consulate whose job was to report the presence of any Bahá'í.

Since Nabíl had Turkish citizenship, the Persian Consul had no legal right to detain him. Nabíl was deceived by being told he was being taken to the Seraye (Governorate) though he was being taken to the house of Consul where he was illegally arrested. However, a Persian traveler, Mírzá Ṣafá, communicated this arbitrary arrest to the Turkish government after which Nabíl was transferred into the hands of the authorities in the port of Alexandria on the Mediterranean Sea.

At this time a very interesting incident occurred. One day, while on the roof of the prison, Nabíl observed a known Bahá'í walking on the street below. The man accompanied by a policeman. Unbeknownst to Nabíl, the Bahá'í who was an acquaintance of Nabíl from Adrianople, was part of the entourage travelling with Bahá'u'lláh on the ship to the prison-city of 'Akká.

At that time, which coincided with the final days of August 1868, Nabíl knew nothing about Bahá'u'lláh's exile to 'Akká. Similarly, Nabíl's whereabouts were known to none. On discovering his friend from the roof of the prison, Nabíl called out to him and in the conversation that ensued Nabíl learned that a steamer carrying Bahá'u'lláh, His family and a group of Bahá'ís to the prison of 'Akká, was at that moment anchored in the harbor. The details of the events that followed are provided by Nabíl:

> I went to Mansuríyyáh[111] by the railway [after arriving from Adrianople], searched for Áqá Siyyid Ḥusayn [of Kashán], found him and told him why I was there. He said that Mírzá Ḥasan Khán, the [Persian] Consul, from the day he managed to send those seven to the Sudán, feared for his life, and had placed spies everywhere that they might inform him whenever a stranger arrived in Egypt.

[110]Title of the Viceroy of Egypt that was at that time part of the Ottoman Empire.

[111]Mansuríyyáh is a town 650 km south of Cairo on the Nile route.

"It is best that you leave your Mathnaví[112] with me, carry nothing of the sacred writings with you, and go to Cairo. There take lodgings at the Takyíy-i-malaví with Shaykh Ibráhím-i-Hamadáni, who receives a stipend from Ismá'il Pasha, and stay until the Khedive [113] returns, when we can find means to send him your Mathnaví."

I went to Cairo, and lodged with Shaykh Ibráhím, not knowing that he was also a spy. One night, in the early hours of the morning, I saw the Blessed Perfection in the world of dreams. He said:

"Some people have come, asking for permission to harm Mírzá Ḥasan Khán; what sayest thou?"

When I awoke I knew that something would happen that day. I went to Sayyid-ná Ḥusayn Square, and walked about for an hour or two. Then I found myself surrounded by a number of people who said,

"They have asked for you at the *Seraye* [Governorate]."

But instead they took me to the house of Mírzá Ḥasan Khán [the Persian Consul]. Then I realized that they had duped me by mentioning the Seraye, so that I should give myself up, and not say that I was not a Persian subject. After long talks with the Consul, I was handed over to an official, who put me in chains. Several times they sent for me. At one time, a number of Persian merchants, such as Mírzá Siyyid Javád-i-Shírází, who was a British subject but presided over the Persians, Hájí Muḥammad Taqíy-Namází and Hájí Muḥammad Ḥasan-i-Kázirúní, were there, seated on chairs, and they made me sit down with them.

However, I was feverish and weakened. They brought a photograph of the Most Great Branch ['Abdu'l-Bahá], and asked me whether I knew who He was. I said:

"Yes, that is the eldest Son of Bahá'u'lláh, Who is known as 'Abbás Effendi ['Abdu'l-Bahá]. I have seen Him many times in

[112]A collection of poems that Nabíl had written for the Khedive.

[113]Title of the Viceroy of Egypt that was at that time part of the Ottoman Empire.

the drawing-room of Khurshíd Pashá, the Válí [Governor] of Adrianople."

They then produced the *Kitáb-i-Íqán*[114] and told me to read to them. I said,

"I have fever and I can't read."

The Consul said,

"He fears to be mocked, should he read."

I replied,

"Let someone else read and I shall have my share of the good deed of mocking."

The book was passed to Hájí Muḥammad Taqíy-Namází. He read the account of the detachment and self-sacrifice of the followers of the Point of the Bayán [the Báb]; if they were not in the right [it asks], then by what proofs could one demonstrate the rightness of the cause of the people of Karbilá. He read on and they kept laughing. Then Mírzá Javád turned to me and asked,

"Why did you become a Bábí? Had the Cause of the Báb been true, I should have become a Bábí, because I am both a Siyyid and a Shirází."[115]

I answered, "But neither has it been proved that I am a Bábí, nor that you are not one. As the poet, Ḥáfiz has it:

From Basrah came Ḥasan, from Ḥabash comes Bilál

From Shám came Ṣuhayb, but from the soil of Mecca

Abú-Jahl; how strange![116]

At that all the people present burst out laughing, and Mírzá Javád became crestfallen. The Consul noticed that the people there had no cause to rejoice, and sent me back to the prison. And I beseeched God never to see him again.

---

[114]The Book Of Certitude revealed by Bahá'u'lláh.

[115]The Báb was both a Siyyid (descendant from Muḥammad) and a native of Shíráz.

[116]Muḥammad and Abú-Jahl, His worst enemy, both came from Mecca. The other three names were from well-distinguished Muslim believers.

That same day he was called to Alexandria on some business. And I had another dream, in which the Blessed Perfection was telling me:

"Within the next eighty-one days, to thee will come some cause of rejoicing."

Then Mírzá Ṣafá arrived from Mecca, and was told that Mírzá Ḥasan Khán had imprisoned a traveller in a dark and dismal .... place.

"Tell him", they said, "for God's sake to free this innocent man."

Mírzá Ṣafá expostulated with him, and telegraphed to have me handed over to the Egyptian authorities and sent to Alexandria. When I was taken there, the late Siyyid Ḥusayn petitioned Sharíf Páshá, and wrote that this traveller was an Ottoman subject whom the Persian consul had unlawfully imprisoned and tortured. Whereupon, I was transferred from the lower to the higher prison. And it was arranged to take the Persian consul to task.

A physician was there in that prison. He tried to convert me to the Protestant Faith. We had long talks and he became a Bahá'í.

On the eighty-first day of my dream, from the roof-top of the prison-house, I caught sight of Áqá Muḥammad-Ibráhím-i-Názír,[117] passing through the street. I called out to him and he came up. I asked him what he was doing there, and he told me that the Blessed Perfection and the companions were being taken to 'Akká ... and that he had come ashore in the company of a policeman to make some purchases.

"The policeman", he said, "will not allow me to stop here much longer. I will go and report your presence here to the Áqá [the Most Great Branch]. Should the ship stay here longer, I shall perhaps come and see you again."

He set my being on fire and went away. The physician was not there at the time. When he came, he found me shedding

[117]A Bahá'í travelling with Bahá'u'lláh being exiled from Gallipoli to 'Akká.

tears, and reciting these lines:

"The Beloved is by my side and I am far away from Him; I am on the shore of the waters of proximity and yet deprived I am. O Friend! Lift me, lift me to a seat on the ship of nearness; I am helpless, I am vanquished, a prisoner am I."

It was in the evening that Fáris (that was the name of the physician) came, and saw my distress. He said,

"You were telling me that on the eighty-first day of your dream, you must receive some cause of rejoicing, and that today was that eighty-first day. Now, on the contrary, I find you greatly disturbed."

I replied,

"Truly that cause for rejoicing has come, but alas! 'The date is on the palm-tree and our hands cannot reach it'".

He said,

"Tell me what has happened, perhaps I could do something about it."

And so I told him that the Blessed Perfection was on that boat. He too, like me, was greatly disturbed, and said

"Were the next day not a Friday[118], and the *Seraye* closed, we could, both of us, have got permission to board the ship and attain His presence. But still, something can be done. You write whatever you wish. I will also write. Tomorrow, one of my acquaintances is coming here. We will get these letters to him to take to the liner."

I wrote my story and gathered together all the poems I had composed in the prison. Fáris, the physician, also wrote a letter and stated his great sorrow. It was very touching. All of these he put in an envelope, which he gave to a young watch-maker named Constantine, to deliver early in the morning. I gave him the name of <u>Kh</u>ádim [Mírzá Áqá Ján] and some others of the companions, told him how to identify them, and impressed on him not to deliver the envelope until he

[118]Friday is the holiday in the Islamic world.

had found one of them. He went out in the morning. We were looking from the roof-top. We first heard the signal, and then the noise of the movement of the ship, and were perplexed, lest he had not made it. Then the ship stopped, and started again after a quarter of an hour. We were on tenterhooks, when suddenly Constantine arrived.

He handed me an envelope and a package in a handkerchief, and exclaimed,

"By God! I saw the Father of Christ."

Fáris, the physician, kissed his eyes and said,

"Our lot was the fire of separation, yours was the bounty of gazing upon the Beloved of the World."

In answer to our petitions, there was a Tablet, in the script of Revelation, a Letter from the Most Great Branch, and a paper filled by almond nuql [a sweet] sent by the Purest Branch. In the Tablet, Fáris, the physician, had been particularly honoured. One of the attendants had written:

"Several times I have witnessed evidences of power which I can never forget. And so it was today. The ship was on the move, when we saw a boat far away. The captain stopped the ship, and this young watch-maker reached us, and called aloud my name. We went to him and he gave us your envelope. All eyes were on us and we are exiles. Yet no one questioned the action of the captain." [119]

In the third volume of *The Revelation of Bahá'u'lláh* the historian Adib Ṭaherzadeh wrote about the Tablet to Fáris:

The Tablet of Bahá'u'lláh was in the handwriting of His amanuensis Mírzá Áqá Ján in the form of 'Revelation Writing'. It imparted a new spirit of love and dedication to Fáris; it fanned into flame the fire of faith which had been ignited in his heart by Nabíl in that gloomy prison. As promised by Bahá'u'lláh, Fáris was released from prison three days later. After his release he arose in the propagation of the Faith

[119]Hasan Balyuzi. *Bahá'u'lláh, the King of Glory.* George Ronald Oxford, 1991, pp. 265-268.

among his people. Nabíl was also freed soon after, but being ordered to leave Egypt he proceeded to the Holy Land in pursuit of his Lord.

In more than one Tablet Bahá'u'lláh has Himself described the episode of Fáris in Alexandria as a token of the power of God. In a Tablet revealed soon after His arrival in 'Akká and addressed to Rada'r-Rúh, a devoted follower from Manshád who died as a martyr, Bahá'u'lláh relates the story of His banishment from Adrianople, and the outpouring of the revelation of the Word of God in the course of that journey; he declares that the breezes of the revelation of the Words revealed in that period wafted over the entire planet. Referring to Himself as the 'Most Great Ocean', He describes in majestic language His boarding the ship and sailing upon the sea, while every drop of its waters was exhilarated and from it could be heard that which no one is capable of hearing.

Perhaps the highlight of this Tablet concerns the story of Fáris. Bahá'u'lláh relates that while the ship was anchored in Alexandria, He received from the hand of a Christian messenger a mighty letter from which He could inhale the fragrances of holiness. It was written by one who had detached himself from worldly ties and embraced His Cause. Bahá'u'lláh states that He wished Rada'r-Rúh had been present to hear the soul-stirring Voice of his Lord as He read aloud to His companions on board the ship the letter of supplication and declaration of faith. This letter, written in Arabic, is indicative of a passionate faith in the Cause of Bahá'u'lláh, a deep understanding of His Revelation and a true recognition of His station. [120]

Bahá'u'lláh ordered copies of parts of the letter of Fáris to be made and sent to certain people in Persia as proof of the power of the Word of God. The letter begins by saying: "O Thou the Glory of the Most Glorious and the Exalted of the Most Exalted! I write this letter and

[120]Adib Taherzadeh. *The Revelation of Bahá'u'lláh,* vol 3. George Ronald Oxford, 1974, pp. 8-9.

present it to the One who has been subjected as Jesus Christ ... It is incumbent upon us to offer praise and thanksgiving to God, the All-glorious, the All-bountiful." [121]

> Fáris may have been the first Christian to accept the Bahá'í Faith.

2.8 In the Holy Land

Ultimately Nabíl-i-A'ẓam was released from prison and subsequently banished to Turkey. Upon learning that a group of Bahá'ís had been transferred to the fortress of Famagusta he left Turkey for the island of Cyprus. Mírzá Yaḥyá had also been included in the decree sending a small group of those associated with Baháu'lláh to Cyprus.

The goal of Nabíl was to attain the presence of Bahá'u'lláh in 'Akká. He may have chosen to access 'Akká from Cyprus for safety reasons as there were strict limitations surrounding the prisoners in 'Akká and visitors thereto. In any case, Nabíl remained only a short time on this island in the Mediterranean. Reaching the fortified citadel of 'Akká in October 1868, three months after the Holy Family's arrival, he found that his Lord was confined in the barracks and all contact with him and fellow exiles was strictly forbidden.

Some followers of Mírzá Yaḥyá, a remnant of the Covenant-breakers, were also sent to 'Akká. Although these two men were included on the exile edict, through conversations with local authorities, they had absolved themselves of the rigors imposed on other exiles in exchange for denouncing all Bahá'ís who attempted to enter the city. They had made their home near the only access gate to the city watching continuously for any followers of Bahá'u'lláh.

When they noticed Nabíl they immediately warned the authorities: "He is a Persian. He is not, as he seems, a man of Bukhárá. He has come here to seek for news of Bahá'u'lláh".[122] Nabíl was intercepted and subjected to interrogation. To the questions posed to him he replied that the reason for his stay was to make some purchases but

---

[121]Adib Taherzadeh. *The Revelation of Bahá'u'lláh,* vol 3. George Ronald Oxford, 1974, pp. 8-9.

[122]'Abdu'l-Bahá. *Memorials of the Faithful.* Wilmette, Bahá'í Publishing Trust, 1971, p.15

his argument was not accepted and he was expelled after only three days in the city. This took place in October 1868.

Overwhelmed with grief, he began to wander through the regions of Galilee, Safá, Hebrón, Nazareth, Haifa, until he later made his home in a cave on Mount Carmel not far from 'Akká. There he lived completely apart from everything, praying and communing with his Lord, longing for the hour of meeting his Beloved. "He lived apart from friend and stranger alike," 'Abdu'l-Bahá said, "lamenting night and day, moaning and chanting prayers." [123]

It has been said that when he arrived in 'Akká and was prevented from reaching Bahá'u'lláh's cell, Nabíl found himself wandering through the surrounding pits of the fortress. Looking up, he suddenly saw the hand of Baha'u'llah extended through the bars of the window expressing His greeting. That same day Nabíl was honored with a prayer specially revealed for him. [124] He was allowed to enter the precincts of the prison for a period of eighty-one days, from 21 March to 9 June 1870, which filled him with joy.

A few months later, Bahá'u'lláh left the barracks to live in a house, but remained nonetheless a prisoner in the city. During the subsequent years, Nabíl had the privilege of residing in the Holy Land and serving his Beloved. 'Abdu'l-Bahá said that when

> ...the gates were flung wide, and the Wronged One issued forth in beauty, in majesty and glory, Nabíl hastened to Him with a joyful heart. Then he used himself up like a candle, burning away with the love of God. Day and night he sang the praises of the one Beloved of both worlds and of those about His threshold, writing verses in the pentameter and hexameter forms, composing lyrics and long odes. Almost daily, he was admitted to the presence of the Manifestation.[125]

At the request of Bahá'u'lláh Nabíl transcribed the text of the Badí'

---

[123]'Abdu'l-Bahá. *Memorials of the Faithful*. Wilmette, Bahá'í Publishing Trust, 1971, p.15

[124]Hasan Balyuzi. *Bahá'u'lláh, the King of Glory*. George Ronald Oxford, 1991.

[125]'Abdu'l-Bahá. *Memorials of the Faithful*. Wilmette, Bahá'í Publishing Trust, 1971, p.15

Calendar created by the Báb for the use of the believers. This was in the year of 1870. According to Nabíl:

> Soon after Bahá'u'lláh had left the fortress of `Akká and was dwelling in the house of Malik, in that city, He commanded me to transcribe the text of the Badí' Calendar and to instruct the believers in its details. On the very day in which I received His command, I composed, in verse and prose, an exposition of the main features of that Calendar and presented it to him.[126]

In January 1872, these years of relative tranquility and close association with the Blessed Perfection, were disturbed by the dishonorable behavior of some Bahá'ís who murdered three Azalís (followers of Mírzá Yaḥyá) with their own hands, ostensibly in pursuit of justice. This incident earned the perpetrators the energetic condemnation of Bahá'u'lláh Himself. The Bahá'í community in the Holy Land had been growing in prestige in the eyes of the local people, and the fame of Bahá'u'lláh's innocence, sanctity and wisdom had spread considerably in the region. However, such an incident tainted the name of the Faith and prompted suffering for Bahá'u'lláh Who was taken to the governorate for interrogation and arrested. Other believers were also imprisoned.

Nabíl and another Bahá'í, Áqá Muḥammad Ḥasan, who were not officially part of the group of exiles were detained for a few days and then forced into exile in Tripoli, near Beirut. Upon his return to the Holy Land, normality and affection from the population to the followers of the Faith returned. It seems that Nabíl made other trips to Iran around 1875 [127]and 1886 [128] engaged in Bahá'í teaching activities at Bahá'u'lláh's requests to confirm the believers in their faith.[129]

---

[126]Bahá'í World Centre. Bahá'í Calendar, Festivals, and Dates of Historic Significance. The *Bahá'í World* (1979-1983), Vol. 18 Haifa, 1986, p. 600.

[127]Moojan Momen. *The Bahá'í Communities of Iran*. George Ronald Oxford, 2015, p. 370 and p. 405.

[128]Moojan Momen. *The Bahá'í Communities of Iran*. George Ronald Oxford, 2015, p. 399.

[129]Hasan Balyuzi. *Eminent Bahá'ís in the Time of Bahá'u'lláh.* George Ronald Oxford, 1985.

It is in the Holy Land that Nabíl began to write his immortal *Narrative*, portions of which were presented to Bahá'u'lláh and 'Abdu'l-Bahá. Nabíl particularly recalls one night when, together with other believers, in the presence of the Blessed Beauty, he had the blessing of hearing from His lips an illustrative account of the history of the Faith.

> Upon the termination of the description of the struggle of Zanján, I was ushered into His presence, and received, together with a number of other believers, the blessings which on two occasions He deigned to confer upon us. Both visits took place during the four days which Bahá'u'lláh chose to tarry in the home of Áqáy-i-Kalím. On the second and fourth nights after His arrival at His brother's house, which fell on the seventh day of the month of Jamádiyu'l-Avval, in the year 1306 A.H., [9 January 1889] I, together with a number of pilgrims from Sarvistán and Fárán, as well as a few resident believers, was admitted into His presence. The words He spoke to us lie forever engraved upon my heart, and I feel it my duty to my readers to share with them the gist of His talk.
>
> "Praise be to God," He said, "that whatever is essential for the believers in this Revelation to be told has been revealed. Their duties have been clearly defined, and the deeds they are expected to perform have been plainly set forth in Our Book. Now is the time for them to arise and fulfil their duty. Let them translate into deeds the exhortations We have given them. Let them beware lest the love they bear God, a love that glows so brightly in their hearts, cause them to transgress the bounds of moderation, and to overstep the limits We have set for them...
>
> Be thankful to God for having enabled you to recognise His Cause. Whoever has received this blessing must, prior to his acceptance, have performed some deed which, though he himself was unaware of its character, was ordained by God as a means whereby he has been guided to find and embrace the Truth. As to those who have remained deprived of such a blessing, their acts alone have hindered them from

> recognising the truth of this Revelation. We cherish the hope that you, who have attained to this light, will exert your utmost to banish the darkness of superstition and unbelief from the midst of the people. May your deeds proclaim your faith and enable you to lead the erring into the paths of eternal salvation. The memory of this night will never be forgotten. May it never be effaced by the passage of time, and may its mention linger for ever on the lips of men." [130]

When Bahá'u'lláh went to live in the Mansion of Bahjí, Nabíl was admitted every Tuesday to the presence of Bahá'u'lláh, an inestimable honor. Nabíl used to live in the city of 'Akká facing the route that the Blessed Beauty followed when He was going to and from the Mansion of Bahjí on His visits to 'Akká. There is a beautiful story told by a believer who along with Nabíl claimed to have a mystical experience while following Bahá'u'lláh from 'Akká to Bahjí.

> On the evening that the Blessed Beauty, exalted be His glory, was to move to the Mansion of Bahjí, this servant and Nabíl-i-A'zam were staying at our residence, which was a room we both shared. It was situated on the upper floor of the Khán-i-Súq-i-Abyad.[131] The room had five glass windows overlooking the road. We were both sitting at the windows looking out, waiting to behold His blessed Person as He passed by. It was nearly two hours after sunset, when we saw Him pass in front of our room riding on a special white donkey. A few steps behind Him, riding on, his donkey, was Khádimu'lláh (the Servant of God) Mírzá Áqá Ján. When He passed out of our sight, Nabíl suggested that we follow Him on foot to the Mansion to circumambulate it and then return home. With much enthusiasm I welcomed the suggestion. We both ran down the stairs immediately and walked quickly behind Him, keeping a distance of about fifty steps. That evening an oil lamp was burning inside the Mansion and we could

---

[130] Nabíl. *The Dawn-Breakers: Nabíl's Narrative of the Early Days of the Bahá'í Revelation.* US Bahá'í Publishing Trust, 1932, pp. 582-586.

[131] An accommodation place near the White Market, the city's main commercial centre.

see its light from outside. It was a very large oil lamp which had three wicks. I was familiar with this lamp because we [Hájí Muḥammad Táhir and Muḥammad Khán-i-Balúch] had brought it with us to the Holy Land. It was presented to the Blessed Beauty by Hájí Siyyid Mírzáy-i-Afnán from Bombay.

When the Blessed Perfection dismounted and went inside the Mansion, we walked toward the building in order to circumambulate. But when we came a little closer we saw to our amazement that the footpaths around the walls of the Mansion were packed with people, who were standing. Crowds had assembled around the four sides of the Mansion and we could hear their murmuring as well as their breathing. Of course we knew that no one had come from 'Akká to circumambulate the Mansion, and we two had gone there without permission. Anyhow, since there was no room to walk on the footpath we stepped back, and at a distance of about thirty steps from the Mansion we circumambulated. To do this we had to walk in some wheatfields and, as it happened, the ground had been recently watered, so we had to walk through muddy fields. As we circled the Mansion we could sense the presence of the multitude on the four sides of the building at some distance from us. In the end we prostrated ourselves on the ground opposite the Gate of the Mansion, and returned to 'Akká. On the way back heavy rain poured down on us, and just as we arrived at the gate of 'Akká, the guards were about to close it. Normally they used to close the gate every night four hours after sunset.

When we arrived home, Nabíl suggested that we ought not to sleep that night and instead keep vigil. He said to me, 'I will compose poems and you make tea.' I made tea several times during the night and Nabíl was engaged in writing poetry. He was a gifted poet, he used to compose extemporaneously. By the morning, he had produced poems written on both sides of a large sheet of paper. We sent a copy of his poems, together with two sugar cones, to the Blessed Beauty. His poems were mainly about history, the history of Bahá'u'lláh's imprisonment, His banishment to

> Baghdád, Istanbul, Adrianople and 'Akká, the sufferings He had endured in the barracks, the story of the building of the Mansion by 'Údí Khammár, and 'Abdu'l-Bahá renting it to serve as a residence for the Blessed Perfection.
>
> He then described the events of the evening Bahá'u'lláh went to the Mansion, and how we both followed Him, the account of our circumambulation when we saw the souls of all the Prophets and Messengers and the Concourse on high assembled outside the Mansion, circumambulating the throne of their Lord. In these poems Nabíl described in detail our keeping vigil, his own writing poems, and my making tea.
>
> When His Blessed Person received the poems of Nabíl, He revealed a Tablet in honour of Nabíl and myself. In it He graciously accepted our pilgrimage to the Mansion, conferred upon Nabíl the title of Bulbul (Nightingale) and upon myself Bahháj (the Blissful). [132]

The day arrived when Bahá'u'lláh ascended to the Realms on High. This occurred in Bahji in the early morning of May 29, 1892. His death was preceded by a short illness in which Nabíl had a private interview with His Holiness. From his words we read:

> Nine months before this event, Bahá'u'lláh once said to 'Abdu'l-Bahá that He did not want to stay longer in this world. From then on, whenever He met with friends, He spoke in a way that everyone felt that His separation was close. With some haste He made the preparations, although He clearly did not say anything.
>
> The night before Sunday, May 8, 1892, He had a slight attack of fever, but He did not reveal it to his friends. The next day He received a few into His presence. In the afternoon the fever had risen and He received only a believer.
>
> On the third day He received me at noon and for half an hour I was honored by His sweet words, walking around the room

[132]Adib Taherzadeh. *The Revelation of Bahá'u'lláh,* vol 4. George Ronald Oxford, 1974, pp. 106-108.

or sitting. Oh! If I had known that this was our last meeting, I would have asked to accept me as a sacrifice to die instead of Him. On the same day a believer came from Egypt and Bahá'u'lláh received him and some other friends. After that no one was allowed to visit him.

All friends were very anxious until the ninth day of his illness in which 'Abdu'l-Bahá came to the Pilgrims' House. He brought Bahá'u'lláh's greetings to everyone and the message that they should not be despair, but rise up to spread the Faith with firmness and constancy; that Bahá'u'lláh always would be with them and they would endure in His thoughts. The words of this message created such a disturbance and sadness that they were about to faint. On Tuesday, the tenth day, we received news of the improvement of the Beloved which filled us all with joy.

On the fifteenth day of his illness, Bahá'u'lláh received in the evening to all who were in the Mansion of Bahjí along with a good number of residents and pilgrims. This was the last interview with His loved ones six days before His Ascension. While resting in His bed, leaning on 'Abdu'l-Bahá gently and affectionately, surrounded by everyone with watery eyes, He addressed the following words:' I am very happy with all of you. You have rendered many services and you have come here. May God assist you to remain united. May He help you to exalt the Cause of the Lord of beings. Then He addressed similar words to the women, including those of His family, who had surrounded His bed. At the end He assured them that in a document entrusted to 'Abdu'l-Bahá He had entrusted them all to his care. [133]

Nabíl could not withstand the weight of his grief. He wrote of the prevailing affliction and of his own pain, after the disappearance of the Lord:

Methinks, the spiritual commotion set up in the world of dust had caused all the worlds of God to tremble... My inner

[133]R. Mehrabkhani. *El Esplendor del Dia Prometido.* Editorial Bahá'í de España, 1974, pp. 377-378.

> and outer tongue are powerless to portray the condition we were in... In the midst of the prevailing confusion a multitude of the inhabitants of 'Akká and of the neighboring villages, that had thronged the fields surrounding the Mansion, could be seen weeping, beating upon their heads, and crying aloud their grief.[134]

These lines, written as a tribute to his Lord, reflect his poignant sentiments:

> O Thou the King of creation and the Ruler of this world and the world to come! Both in Thy presence and in Thy absence, Thou hast been the cause of the tranquillity of the hearts of men and the advancement of the nations. From the moment Thou didst mount Thy throne at the hour of dawn on the 2nd on Muharram 1233 (12 November 1817) until Thy Ascension to the Realms of Eternity, eight hours after sunset on the 2nd of Dhi'l-Qa'dih 1309 (29 May 1892) a period of seventy-seven years less two months according to the lunar calendar...Thou wert at all times, at day and at night, each month and each year, the cause of the exaltation of mankind. No needy suppliant who had set his heart toward Thee was turned back from the door of Thy generosity without vouchsafing unto him supreme felicity and goodly gifts, and no sorrowful destitute was sent out of Thy All-glorious presence except that Thou didst bestow upon him blissful joy and ample hope. And now far be it from Thee not to relieve me from my dreadful woes, and lead me to the abode of a never-ending felicity. Thou art God and there is no God save Thee.[135]

'Abdu'l-Bahá commissioned Nabíl to select passages from the Writings that now constitute the Table of Visitation which is read at

[134]Shoghi Effendi. *God Passes By.* US Bahá'í Publishing Trust, 1979, p. 222.

[135]Adib Taherzadeh. *The Revelation of Bahá'u'lláh*, vol 4. George Ronald Oxford, 1974, pp. 418-419.

the Shrine of Bahá'u'lláh.[136] This work may have been given to him to calm his distress and sadness and thus distract him from the idea of seeking death.[137]

Nabíl loved 'Abdu'l-Bahá very much. But the intensity of his pain over the disappearance of his Beloved led him to take his own life by drowning in the waters of the Mediterranean Sea, on whose beaches, shortly afterwards, he was found lifeless.

The epitaph on his tomb, extracted from one of his last poems, expresses his feelings:

> Nabíl hath been immersed in the ocean
>
> of the Mercy of his Glorious Lord.
>
> Open Thou a way for a consumed heart to see,
>
> Drowned — drowned in this year let me be![138]

Before the day he decided to take flight to his Beloved, he wrote an elegy in homage to 'Abdu'l-Bahá in which he refers to the date of his death and to his decision. He wrote the word "Gharíq" which means "drowned". The numerical value of this word according to the abjad art comes to 1,310 that in the Muslim calendar gives us the year 1892. In one of his odes he concludes: "The Lord has departed from this world". Again, the numerical value of the expression gives us the year 1892.

Nothing is more eloquent and enlightening than these words of 'Abdu'l-Bahá, with which he closes a short biography of the life of Yár-Muḥammad Zarandí, the simple shepherd who became the Greatest Nobleman of the Bahá'í Faith:

> Throughout all his life, from earliest youth till he was feeble and old, he spent his time serving and worshiping

---

[136] Marzieh Gail. *Dawn Over Mount Hira and Other Essays.* George Ronald Oxford, 1976. Available online at: https://bahai-library.com/pdf/g/gail_dawn_mount_hira.pdf

[137] Vahid Rafati, NABIL-E AʿẒAM ZARANDI, MOLLĀ MOḤAMMAD. *Encyclopædia Iranica*, online edition, 2016, available at http://www.iranicaonline.org/articles/nabil-zarandi (accessed on 29 June 2019).

[138] David S. Ruhe. *Door of Hope: A Century of the Bahá'í Faith in the Holy Land.* George Ronald Oxford, 1983, p. 91

> the Lord. He bore hardships, he lived through misfortunes, he suffered afflictions. From the lips of the Manifestation he heard marvelous things. He was shown the lights of Paradise; he won his dearest wish. And at the end, when the Daystar of the world had set, he could endure no more, and flung himself into the sea. The waters of sacrifice closed over him; he was *drowned*, and he came, at last, to the Most High. Upon him be abundant blessings; upon him be tender mercies. May he win a great victory, and a manifest grace in the Kingdom of God. [139]

3. Tablets to Nabíl

Nabíl was graced with several Tablets from Bahá'u'lláh. Among those that stand out is the Súriy-i-Damm (Tablet of Blood), a valuable document in the Arabic language, most likely revealed when Nabíl returned from a teaching trip in Persia and had once again reached the presence of Bahá'u'lláh in Adrianople. According to the historian Adib Taherzadeh:

> In the Súriy-i-Damm Bahá'u'lláh counsels Nabíl to adorn himself with His characteristics, to waft the musk-laden breeze of holiness upon the believers and to bear with resignation and fortitude the sufferings and persecutions which may be inflicted upon him. He exhorts him to be resigned and submissive when sorely oppressed, reminds him that resignation and submission are among His own attributes and states that of all deeds there is nothing more meritorious in the estimation of God than the sighs of one wronged and oppressed who endures suffering with patience and fortitude. He urges Nabíl to seek the companionship of the loved ones of God wherever he goes, to appear among the people with dignity and serenity, to teach the Cause of His Lord in accordance with the capacity of those who hear him, and to rely upon God for His assistance and confirmations.[140]

[139] 'Abdu'l-Bahá. *Memorials of the Faithful.* Wilmette, Bahá'í Publishing Trust, 1971, pp. 35-36.

[140] Adib Taherzadeh. *The Revelation of Bahá'u'lláh*, vol 2. George Ronald Oxford, 1974, p. 238.

Below are some passages of the Súriy-i-Damm, in which the essential unity of the divine Messengers is enunciated and the concept of through the Progressive Revelation of God to the world.

> Praise be to Thee, O Lord My God, for the wondrous revelations of Thy inscrutable decree and the manifold woes and trials Thou hast destined for Myself. At one time Thou didst deliver Me into the hands of Nimrod; at another Thou hast allowed Pharaoh's rod to persecute Me. Thou, alone, canst estimate, through Thine all-encompassing knowledge and the operation of Thy Will, the incalculable afflictions I have suffered at their hands. Again Thou didst cast Me into the prison-cell of the ungodly, for no reason except that I was moved to whisper into the ears of the well-favored denizens of Thy Kingdom an intimation of the vision with which Thou hadst, through Thy knowledge, inspired Me, and revealed to Me its meaning through the potency of Thy might. And again Thou didst decree that I be beheaded by the sword of the infidel. Again I was crucified for having unveiled to men's eyes the hidden gems of Thy glorious unity, for having revealed to them the wondrous signs of Thy sovereign and everlasting power. How bitter the humiliations heaped upon Me, in a subsequent age, on the plain of Karbilá! How lonely did I feel amidst Thy people! To what a state of helplessness I was reduced in that land! Unsatisfied with such indignities, My persecutors decapitated Me, and, carrying aloft My head from land to land paraded it before the gaze of the unbelieving multitude, and deposited it on the seats of the perverse and faithless. In a later age, I was suspended, and My breast was made a target to the darts of the malicious cruelty of My foes. My limbs were riddled with bullets, and My body was torn asunder. Finally, behold how, in this Day, My treacherous enemies have leagued themselves against Me, and are continually plotting to instill the venom of hate and malice into the souls of Thy servants. With all their might they are scheming to accomplish their purpose.... Grievous as is My plight, O God, My Well-Beloved, I render thanks unto Thee, and My Spirit is grateful for whatsoever hath befallen

> me in the path of Thy good-pleasure. I am well pleased with that which Thou didst ordain for Me, and welcome, however calamitous, the pains and sorrows I am made to suffer.[141]

There is another beautiful and significant Tablet of Bahá'u'lláh addressed to Nabíl, also translated by the Guardian of the Faith, containing exhortations to all the members of humanity:

> Let thine ear be attentive, O Nabíl-i-'Aẓam, to the Voice of the Ancient of Days, crying to thee from the Kingdom of His all-glorious Name. He it is Who is now proclaiming from the realms above, and within the inmost essence of all created things: "I truly am God, there is none other God but Me. I am He Who, from everlasting, hath been the Source of all sovereignty and power, He Who shall continue, throughout eternity, to exercise His kingship and to extend His protection unto all created things. My proof is the greatness of My might and My sovereignty that embraceth the whole of creation." ...
>
> Blessed art thou, O My name, inasmuch as thou hast entered Mine Ark, and art speeding, through the power of My sovereign and most exalted might, on the ocean of grandeur, and art numbered with My favored ones whose names the Finger of God hath inscribed. Thou hast quaffed the cup which is life indeed from the hands of this Youth, around Whom revolve the Manifestations of the All-Glorious, and the brightness of Whose presence they Who are the Day Springs of Mercy extol in the day time and in the night season.
>
> His glory be with thee, inasmuch as thou hast journeyed from God unto God, and entered within the borders of the Court of unfading splendor—the Spot which mortal man can never describe. Therein hath the breeze of holiness, laden with the love of thy Lord, stirred thy spirit within thee, and the waters of understanding have washed from thee the stains of remoteness and ungodliness. Thou hast gained admittance into the Paradise of God's Remembrance, through thy recognition of Him Who is the Embodiment of

[141]Bahá'u'lláh. *Gleanings from the Writings of Bahá'u'lláh.* US Bahá'í Publishing Trust, 1990, pp. 88-89.

that Remembrance amongst men.

Wherefore, be thankful to God, for having strengthened thee to aid His Cause, for having made the flowers of knowledge and understanding to spring forth in the garden of thine heart. Thus hath His grace encompassed thee, and encompassed the whole of creation. Beware, lest thou allow anything whatsoever to grieve thee. Rid thyself of all attachment to the vain allusions of men, and cast behind thy back the idle and subtle disputations of them that are veiled from God. Proclaim, then, that which the Most Great Spirit will inspire thee to utter in the service of the Cause of thy Lord, that thou mayest stir up the souls of all men and incline their hearts unto this most blessed and all-glorious Court....

Know thou that We have annulled the rule of the sword, as an aid to Our Cause, and substituted for it the power born of the utterance of men. Thus have We irrevocably decreed, by virtue of Our grace. Say: O people! Sow not the seeds of discord among men, and refrain from contending with your neighbor, for your Lord hath committed the world and the cities thereof to the care of the kings of the earth, and made them the emblems of His own power, by virtue of the sovereignty He hath chosen to bestow upon them. He hath refused to reserve for Himself any share whatever of this world's dominion. To this He Who is Himself the Eternal Truth will testify. The things He hath reserved for Himself are the cities of men's hearts, that He may cleanse them from all earthly defilements, and enable them to draw nigh unto the hallowed Spot which the hands of the infidel can never profane. Open, O people, the city of the human heart with the key of your utterance. Thus have We, according to a pre-ordained measure, prescribed unto you your duty.

By the righteousness of God! The world and its vanities, and its glory, and whatever delights it can offer, are all, in the sight of God, as worthless as, nay, even more contemptible than, dust and ashes. Would that the hearts of men could comprehend it! Cleanse yourselves thoroughly, O people of Bahá, from the defilement of the world, and of all that pertaineth unto it. God Himself beareth Me witness. The things of the earth ill beseem you. Cast them away unto such as may desire them, and fasten your eyes upon this most holy and effulgent Vision.

That which beseemeth you is the love of God, and the love of Him Who is the Manifestation of His Essence, and the observance of whatsoever He chooseth to prescribe unto you, did ye but know it.

Say: Let truthfulness and courtesy be your adorning. Suffer not yourselves to be deprived of the robe of forbearance and justice, that the sweet savors of holiness may be wafted from your hearts upon all created things. Say: Beware, O people of Bahá, lest ye walk in the ways of them whose words differ from their deeds. Strive that ye may be enabled to manifest to the peoples of the earth the signs of God, and to mirror forth His commandments. Let your acts be a guide unto all mankind, for the professions of most men, be they high or low, differ from their conduct. It is through your deeds that ye can distinguish yourselves from others. Through them the brightness of your light can be shed upon the whole earth. Happy is the man that heedeth My counsel, and keepeth the precepts prescribed by Him Who is the All-Knowing, the All-Wise. [142]

[142]Bahá'u'lláh. *Gleanings from the Writings of Bahá'u'lláh.* US Bahá'í Publishing Trust, 1990, pp. 301-304.

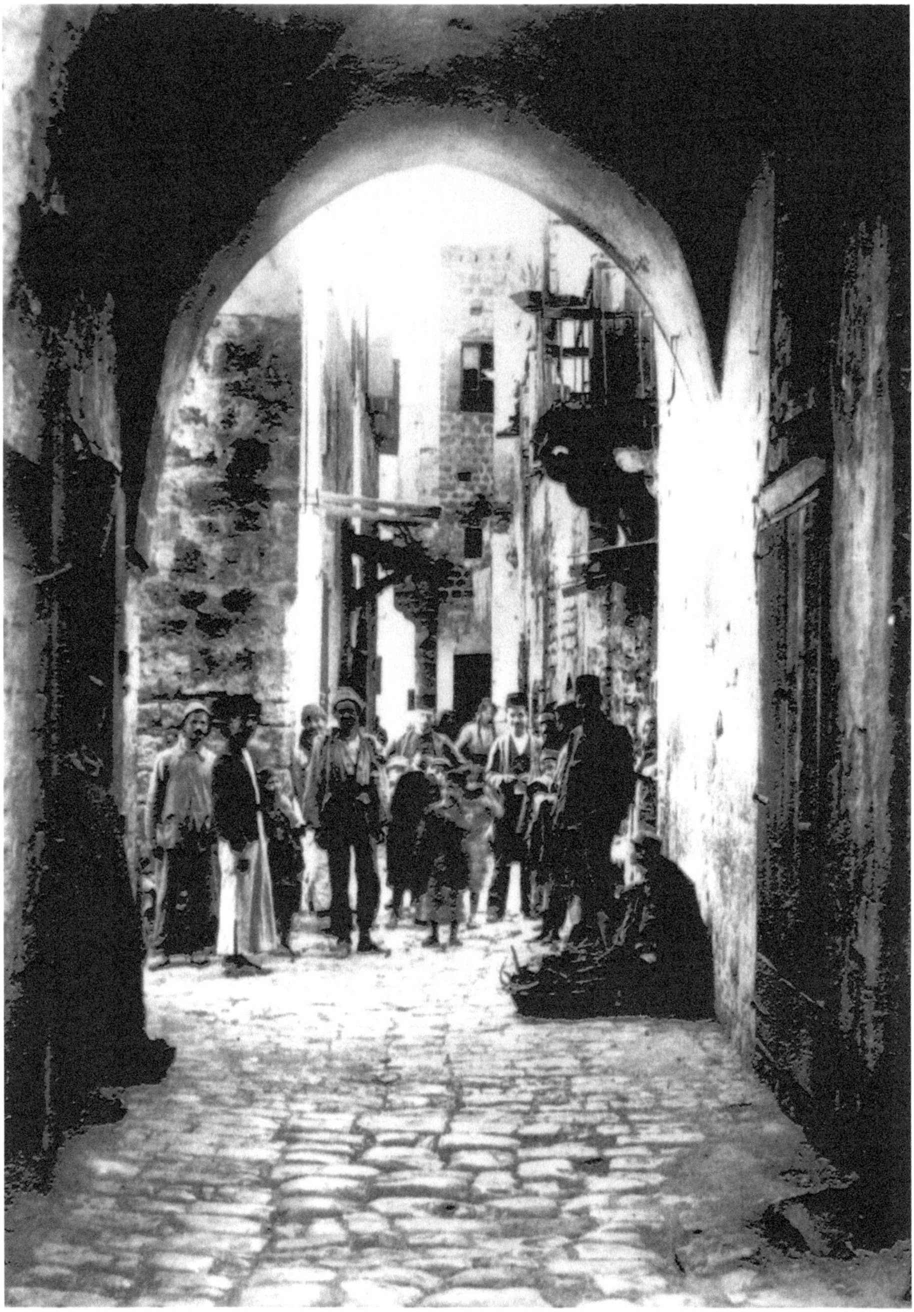

Figure 8: A street in 'Akká c. 1914.
Courtesy: Bahá'í Media

Figure 9: The House of 'Abbúd in 'Akká where Bahá'u'lláh resided.
Courtesy: Bahá'í Media

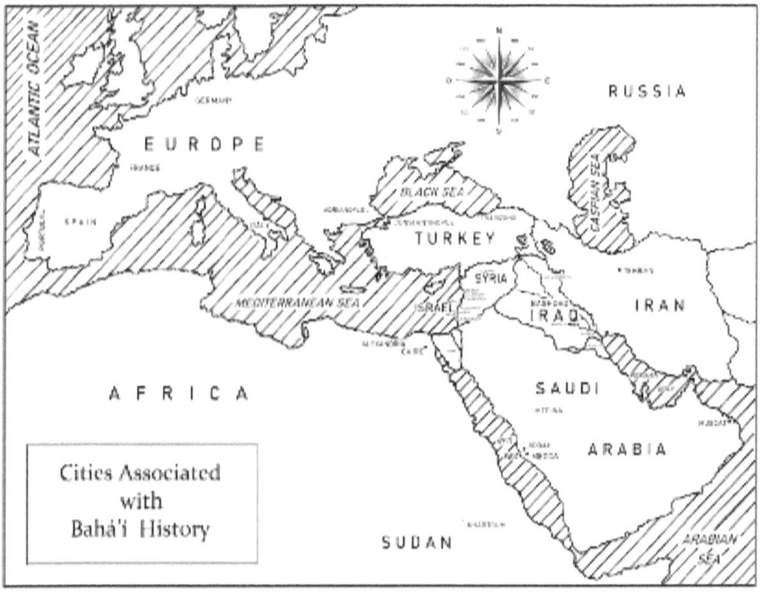

Figure 10: Cities associated with Bahá'í history.
Courtesy: Pedro Donaires

Figure 11: Ibn-i-Aṣdaq, son of Mullá Ṣádiq

Figure 12: A view of Baghdad in the nineteenth century.
Courtesy: Bahá'í Media

Figure 13: Original corridor to the entrance of the Síyáh-Chál in Tehran

Figure 14: Aerial view of city of 'Akká, May 1972. Courtesy: Bahá'í Media

Mullá Ṣádiq

THE HAND OF THE CAUSE OF GOD ENTITLED ISMULLÁHU'L AṢDAQ —THE NAME OF GOD, THE TRUE—

How great is the Cause, how staggering the weight of its Message![143]

Bahá'u'lláh

[143]Shoghi Effendi. *The Advent of Divine Justice.* US Bahá'í Publishing Trust, 1990, p. 77.

1. Paving the Way

Mullá Muḥammad-Ṣádiq-i-Khurásání, or Mullá Ṣádiq as he is better known, was so renowned for his spirituality that Bahá'ís and non-Bahá'ís alike called him *Muqqadas* (the Saint). This chapter will explore the great piety, zeal and service of Mullá Ṣádiq to the Báb and Bahá'u'lláh.

He was born in 1799, the son of Mírzá Ismá'íl into a renowned clerical family from Mahshad, the capital of Khurásán province, northeast of Iran.[144] Because of his deep knowledge of Islamic jurisprudence, he had been elevated to the high rank of *muhtajid.*

Bahá'u'lláh conferred upon him the title "Ismu'lláhu'l Aṣdaq", an Arabic title which translates into English as "the Name of God, the True One". After his death, 'Abdu'-l-Bahá posthumously named him a Hand of the Cause of God. Mullá Ṣádiq served the Faith of God with exemplary devotion during the ministries of the Báb and Bahá'u'lláh. The Blessed Beauty referred to him and his son as martyrs, even though both died of natural causes in 1889 and 1928, respectively.[145]

When he embraced the Cause of God, Mullá Ṣádiq became a true teacher of the Bahá'í Teachings. In His book *Memorials of the Faithful,* 'Abdu'l-Bahá also said that he "was truly a servant of the Lord from the beginning of life till his last breath."[146]

Mullá Ṣádiq was born into a prominent family in the province of Khurásán, Persia. As a young man he was interested in the study of theology and achieved a mastery of those subjects. He was highly regarded for his piety and good character, becoming well-known in the religious circles of 'Iráq, a neighboring country to Iran. He went to that country to study Islamic sciences around 1830.

While still young, Mullá Ṣádiq enrolled in the school of the

---

[144]Dominic Parviz Brookshaw. Letters to Bahá'í princesses: Tablets revealed in honour of the women of Ibn-i Aṣdaq's household. L*ights of Irfan,* volume 5, 2003, pp. 17-40. Available on line at: http://irfancolloquia.org/pdf/lights5_brookshaw.pdf

[145]Hasan Balyuzi. *Eminent Bahá'ís in the Time of Bahá'u'lláh.* George Ronald Oxford, 1985, p. 171.

[146]'Abdu'l-Bahá. *Memorials of the Faithful.* Wilmette, Bahá'í Publishing Trust, 1971, p. 5.

distinguished scholar Shaykh Aḥmad and his successor Siyyid Káẓim. Their teachings became known as the Shaykhí School. These "twin resplendent lights" [147] as Bahá'u'lláh called them, had started a mystical movement that preached the symbolic interpretation of the term used in the prophecies such as "resurrection", the "coming", "heaven ", among others, and also announced the imminent coming of the Messenger promised in all religions of the past. Siyyid Káẓim selected some of his best students and focused on extending their knowledge. One of them was Mullá Ṣádiq.

Mullá Ṣádiq had the blessing of meeting the Báb before His revelation in the city of Karbila while visiting the Shrine of Imam Ḥusayn. According to Hasan Balyuzi:

> Mullá Ṣádiq, enamoured as he was of the mien and the bearing of that young Siyyid [the Báb], Whom he had encountered facing the Shrine of the Third Imam [Ḥusayn], had, one day, ventured to speak to Him and invite Him to visit his house, where Siyyid Káẓim was expected to attend a Rawdih-Khaní, an assemblage devoted to the recital of the sufferings of the House of the Prophet, and particularly the martyrdom of the Third Imam. The young Siyyid had readily and graciously accepted the invitation. When Mírzá 'Alí-Muḥammad [The Báb], that young Siyyid of Shíráz, arrived at Mullá Ṣádiq's house, Siyyid Káẓim and his disciples were already there and seated. On seeing the young Shírázi make His entrance, Siyyid Káẓim immediately rose and asked Him to take a seat much higher in the room. Those present were amazed and speechless because of the marked respect shown by Siyyid Káẓim to this very young Siyyid, Who was unknown in their circles in Karbilá.
>
> A few days later, Siyyid 'Alí-Muḥammad once again encountered Mullá Ṣádiq in the compound of the Shrine of the Third Imam. He told him that His uncle had arrived from Shíráz and asked whether Mullá Ṣádiq wished to meet him. That afternoon Mullá Ṣádiq visited the house where Siyyid 'Alí-Muḥammad lodged. He found that His uncle had many visitors: Persians of high rank, divines and merchants.

[147] Bahá'u'lláh. *The Kitáb-i-Íqán.* US Bahá'í Publishing Trust, 1989, p.65.

Siyyid 'Alí-Muḥammad Himself was busy dispensing tea and other refreshments. Mullá Ṣádiq was soon expressing to the S͟hírází merchant the unbounded admiration which he cherished for his Nephew, so unique in every way. Hájí Mírzá Siyyid 'Alí was glad to hear a total stranger speak in such glowing terms of his Nephew and replied: 'In S͟híráz all the members of our family are well known for their outstanding qualities, but my young Nephew is unique and excels them all. But despite His high qualities, He falls short in one way. He neglects His studies.' Mullá Ṣádiq responded that should the young man be kept in Karbila, he himself would undertake to supervise His studies, to which offer Hájí Mírzá Siyyid 'Alí readily agreed. However, soon after, both he and his remarkable Nephew returned to S͟híráz. [148]

During his lifetime, Siyyid Káẓim instructed Mullá Ṣádiq to reside in the city of Iṣfahán to prepare people for the coming of the Promised One. When his master died on the last day of 1843, Mullá Ṣádiq had been living in that city for nearly five years. Far from being discouraged, Mullá Ṣádiq continued talking to others about the upcoming advent of the Messenger of God.

In May of 1844 Siyyid 'Alí Muḥammad, Who came to be known by the title of the "Gate" declared at the age of twenty-five years of age that God had chosen Him to be the mouthpiece of a new divine revelation. The scene of such a wondrous revelation was the city of S͟híráz. The first disciple was Mullá Ḥusayn who along with seventeen of Siyyid Káẓim's students that had also accepted the Báb, became known as the Letters of the Living. They are considered the first Bábís of Persia.

All except one had the inestimable privilege of attaining the presence of the Báb. At His bidding they left the city of S͟híráz heading toward their home provinces to commence their apostolic work of spreading the Good News that God had manifested Himself again.

The new teachings attracted fierce persecution particularly as they were considered a heresy by the ecclesiastical establishment who,

---

[148]Hasan Balyuzi. *Eminent Bahá'ís in the Time of Bahá'u'lláh.* George Ronald Oxford, 1985, pp. 8-9

joining forces with the Iranian government, committed themselves to the eradication of the Faith of the Báb.

2. Accepting the New Faith

It was around this time that Mullá Ḥusayn passed through the city of Iṣfahán. Mullá Ṣádiq was still living in that region determined to fulfill the task of preparing the hearts of the people for the coming of the Day of God. He did not know anything about the arrival of the Báb's first disciple until Mullá Ḥusayn went to visit Mullá Ṣádiq who in the same night joyfully acknowledged the truth of the Báb's revelation.

Years later, Mullá Ṣádiq spoke of what happened in that unforgettable encounter:

> I asked Mullá Ḥusayn to divulge the name of Him who claimed to be the promised Manifestation. He replied:
>
> 'To enquire about that name and to divulge it are alike forbidden.'
>
> 'Would it, then, be possible,' I asked, 'for me, even as the Letters of the Living, to seek independently the grace of the All-Merciful and, through prayer, to discover His identity?'
>
> 'The door of His grace,' he replied, 'is never closed before the face of him who seeks to find Him.'
>
> I immediately retired from his presence, and requested his host to allow me the privacy of a room in his house where, alone and undisturbed, I could commune with God. In the midst of my contemplation, I suddenly remembered the face of a Youth whom I had often observed while in Karbilá, standing in an attitude of prayer, with His face bathed in tears at the entrance of the shrine of the Imám Ḥusayn. That same countenance now reappeared before my eyes. In my vision I seemed to behold that same face, those same features, expressive of such joy as I could never describe. He smiled as He gazed at me. I went towards Him, ready to throw myself at His feet. I was bending towards the ground, when, lo! that radiant figure vanished from before me. Overpowered with joy and gladness, I ran out to meet Mullá Ḥusayn, who with transport received me and assured me that I had, at last,

> attained the object of my desire. He bade me, however, to repress my feelings.
>
> 'Declare not your vision to anyone,' he urged me; 'the time for it has not yet arrived. You have reaped the fruit of your patient waiting in Iṣfahán. You should now proceed to Kirmán, and there acquaint Ḥájí Mírzá Karím Khán with this Message. From that place you should travel to Shíráz and endeavour to rouse the people of that city from their heedlessness. I hope to join you in Shíráz and share with you the blessings of a joyous reunion with our Beloved.' [149]

Such an experience awakened his heart and he became fully attracted by the fragrances of the Faith of the Báb. However, it was not until Mullá Ṣádiq reached Shíráz that he embraced the Cause of God.

He would later meet the Báb and receive from Him the designation of "Witness of the Bayán" — a very elevated position within the hierarchy of the Báb's Dispensation. Because of this rank Mullá Ṣádiq was commissioned to guarantee the authenticity and validity of the Bayán (the Báb's Book of Laws) until the appearance of "Him Whom God Will Make Manifest" (Bahá'u'lláh). The Báb's main mission was to prepare the way for a greater Messenger of God who within a decade would follow, to guide humanity to its golden age, referred to in religious traditions as the Day of God. It has been said that when Mullá Ṣádiq saw the Báb for the first time he exclaimed: "Glorified be our Lord, the Most High". [150]

When he arrived in Shíráz, Mullá Ṣádiq began to speak publicly about the prophecies concerning the appearance of the Báb. Nobody could refute him because in that field he was the teacher of teachers.

> The people of Khurásán were strongly attached to him, for he was a great scholar and among the most renowned of matchless and unique divines. As a teacher of the Faith, he spoke with such eloquence, such extraordinary power, that

---

[149]Nabíl. *The Dawn-Breakers: Nabíl's Narrative of the Early Days of the Bahá'í Revelation.* US Bahá'í Publishing Trust, 1932, pp. 100-101.

[150]Adib Taherzadeh. *The Revelation of Bahá'u'lláh*, vol 3. George Ronald Oxford, 1974, p. 254

his hearers were won over with great ease. [151]

To Mullá Ṣádiq's delight, Quddús, one of the Letters of the Living, arrived in Shíráz. Quddus was a young man of profound knowledge and piety who had previously undertaken a pilgrimage to Mecca with the Báb. When they returned to Persia, the Báb stayed in the port of Bushir for a while whereas Quddus was sent to Shíráz. The Báb Himself returned to Shíráz in June 1845. When parting, Quddus was told:

> The days of your companionship with Me are drawing to a close. The hour of separation has struck, a separation which no reunion will follow except in the Kingdom of God, in the presence of the King of Glory. In this world of dust, no more than nine fleeting months of association with Me have been allotted to you. On the shores of the Great Beyond, however, in the realm of immortality, joy of eternal reunion awaits us. The hand of destiny will ere long plunge you into an ocean of tribulation for His sake. I, too, will follow you; I, too, will be immersed beneath its depths. Rejoice with exceeding gladness, for you have been chosen as the standard-bearer of the host of affliction, and are standing in the vanguard of the noble army that will suffer martyrdom in His name. In the streets of Shíráz, indignities will be heaped upon you, and the severest injuries will afflict your body. You will survive the ignominious behaviour of your foes, and will attain the presence of Him who is the one object of our adoration and love. In His presence you will forget all the harm and disgrace that shall have befallen you. The hosts of the Unseen will hasten forth to assist you, and will proclaim to all the world your heroism and glory. Yours will be the ineffable joy of quaffing the cup of martyrdom for His sake. I, too, shall tread the path of sacrifice, and will join you in the realm of eternity.[152]

[151]'Abdu'l-Bahá. *Memorials of the Faithful.* Wilmette, Bahá'í Publishing Trust, 1971, pp. 5-6.

[152]Nabíl. *The Dawn-Breakers: Nabíl's Narrative of the Early Days of the Bahá'í Revelation.* US Bahá'í Publishing Trust, 1932, pp. 142-143.

What follows is the story of Mullá Ṣádiq who along with Quddús and another believer Mullá 'Alí-Akbar, were among the first to suffer persecution for the Cause of God on Persian soil.

A major event occurred when Quddús handed to Mullá Ṣádiq a treaty composed by the Báb called the "Dalá'il-i-Sab'ih" (the Seven Proofs). In this book the Báb pointed out the essential requirements of a true believer in His Faith. At the same time, the Báb exhorted each of them to modify the Adhán, the official religious call to congregational prayer, adding an innovative verse: "I bear witness that He whose name is 'Alí-Qabl-i-Muḥammad is the servant of the Baqíyyatu'lláh." [153] With this expression the Báb alluded to Himself and Bahá'u'lláh, respectively. For the Muslim hierarchy, the new call represented a heretical statement. Those who spoke such words were to be punished and repressed.

Mullá Ṣádiq became so enthusiastic by the Báb's treatise that in one of the main city mosques where he had become a *imám jum'a*, that is, a leader of congregational prayers, he began to recite the new call to a surprised congregation.[154] As soon as he finished, the divines rose from their front row protesting the change of ritual. They claimed heresy and began inflaming the crowd demanding a severe chastisement.

In their clamor, the clergy claimed that the integrity of the Faith of Muḥammad was being destroyed. The commotion was such that the fury overflowed the precincts of the temple and, exacerbated by the hysterical complaints of the priests, spread throughout the city. In their cries they asked for the punishment of Mullá Ṣádiq.

The governor of the province was also affected by the riots that threatened to disrupt public order. He was informed that a citizen of Shíráz - the Báb — had declared to be God's spokesman. He was told the Báb remained in Bushir and was given information about the activities of His followers. He was told that the Báb was exhorting

[153]Nabíl. *The Dawn-Breakers: Nabíl's Narrative of the Early Days of the Bahá'í Revelation*. US Bahá'í Publishing Trust, 1932, p. 144.

[154]Dominic Parviz Brookshaw. Letters to Bahá'í princesses: Tablets revealed in honour of the women of Ibn-i Aṣdaq's household. *Lights of Irfan*, volume 5, 2003, pp. 17-40. Available on line at: http://irfancolloquia.org/pdf/lights5_brookshaw.pdf

all Muslims to embrace His Faith as a matter of a true believer's duty.

The governor, incited by the local clergy, arrested Quddús and Mullá Ṣádiq, and most likely Mullá 'Alí-Akbar at the same time. In shackles the prisoners were taken to the governor. Because Quddús was young and of mild appearance, the authority turned its anger towards Mullá Ṣádiq who was much older.

This governor had read the first paragraphs of the Qayyúmu'l-Asmá' a book of the Báb that was snatched from Mullá Ṣádiq by the police when he was reading, passionately and loudly, to the congregation. In this book, the Báb addressed the kings and rulers of the earth urging them to give up their earthly sovereignty.

Upon reading it, the governor became confused by such emphatic terms. He furiously asked Mullá Ṣádiq if those terms also referred to and should be applied to the Sháh of Persia, and to his own sovereignty given that he was the governor of the province. Mullá Ṣádiq replied that such was the case because this was the Word of God and it did not matter whether it was the Sháh or any other monarch - the divine purpose cannot be altered.

Mullá Ṣádiq's uncompromising answer angered the governor who insulted and cursed Mullá Ṣádiq. As a manifestation of his implacable rage the governor ordered that Mullá Ṣádiq's and Quddús' noses be pierced and a string be passed through the holes thus created. They were then taken through the streets of the city, and exposed to the insults and jeers of the populace. According to the historian Nabíl, the governor was not satisfied with that cruelty. He further ordered the burning of their beards. Orders were given for Mullá Ṣádiq to be undressed and given a thousand lashes.

Resigned to his fate, but happy to suffer tribulation in the path of God, Mullá Ṣádiq recited some words from the Qur'án:

> O Lord, our God! We have indeed heard the voice of One that called. He called us to the Faith—'Believe ye on the Lord your God!'—and we have believed. O God, our God! Forgive us, then, our sins, and hide away from us our evil deeds, and cause us to die with the righteous. [155]

[155]Nabíl. *The Dawn-Breakers: Nabíl's Narrative of the Early Days of the Bahá'í Revelation*. US Bahá'í Publishing Trust, 1932, pp. 146-147.

Despite his advanced age and the fragility of his body, no one protested or stopped the harshness of the torment. He was stripped naked and the executioners took turns to inflict their violence on his bleeding back.

A person among the crowd admired Mullá Ṣádiq's strength noticing that, while the torture was taking place, he would cover his mouth as if he left no pain from those painful blows. Shortly after, Mullá Ṣádiq reported that the first seven blows were very painful, but from the next until the last one was over, he had lost the sensation of the effect of the lashes. He himself marveled at the truth of the statement that the pains and sufferings in God's way become joy.

The unfortunate group was driven out of the city, but not before threatening them with crucifixion should they return. Mullá Ṣádiq was a guest of the Báb for ten days, and then left the city.[156]

3. An Excellent Global Proclamation

Bahá'u'lláh has expressed in His Writings that, "The movement itself from place to place, when undertaken for the sake of God, hath always exerted, and can now exert, its influence in the world." [157]

The wisdom of these words is evidenced by the effects of this first persecution of the Faith of God in Persia. A few months later an article appeared in *The Times of London*, the most widely read Western newspaper, with the first reference to the advent of the Báb in the Christian world.

In its regular edition of 1 November 1845, an article was published under the title "Persia" which described the journey of the Báb to Mecca, His arrival in Persia and suffering of the Bábís in Shíraz. "For as the lightning comes from the east and shines as far as the west"[158], that news illuminated the continents of Europe and America, as well as other places in the world, with the proclamation of the Báb. The

[156]Vahid Rafati. ḴORĀSĀNI, MOLLĀ ṢĀDEQ. Encyc*lopædia Iranica,* online edition, 2016, available at http://www.iranicaonline.org/articles/khorasani-molla-sadeq (accessed on 29 June 2019).

[157]Shoghi Effendi. *The Advent of Divine Justice.* US Bahá'í Publishing Trust, 1990, p. 84.

[158]Matthew 24:27.

article reads as follows:

> We have been favored with the following letter, dated for Bushire, August 10:
>
> A Persian merchant, who has lately returned from a pilgrimage to Mecca, had been for sometime endeavouring here to prove that he was one of the successors of Mohamet [Muḥammad], and therefore had a right to demand of all true Mussulmans to mention him as such in their profession of faith; he had already collected a good number of followers, who secretly aided him in forwarding his views. On the evening of the 23rd June last, I have been informed from a creditable source, four persons being heard at Shíráz repeating their profession of faith according to the form prescribed by the new impostor were apprehended, tried, and found guilty of unpardonable blasphemy. They were sentenced to lose their beards by fire being set to them. The sentence was put into execution with all the zeal and fanaticism becoming a true believer of Mohamet. Not deeming the loss of beards a sufficient punishment for the believers in the impostor, they were further sentenced on the next day to have their faces blacked and exposed throughout the city. Each of them was led by a Mirgazah (executioner), who had made a hole in his nose and passed through it a string, which he sometimes pulled with such violence that the unfortunate felloes cried out alternately for mercy from the executioner and for vengeance from Heaven. It is the custom in Persia on such occasions for the executioners to collect money from the spectators, and particularly from the shopkeepers in the bazaar. In the evening, when the pockets of the executioners were well filled with money, they led the unfortunate fellows to the city gate, and there told them
>
> The world was all before them where to choose
>
> Their place of rest, and Providence their guide.'
>
> After which the Mollahs[159] at Shíráz sent the men to Bushire with power to seize the impostor, and take him

[159]Muslim clergy.

> to Shíráz, where, on being tried, he very wisely denied the charge of apostacy laid against him and thus escaped from punishment.[160]

The story includes misinformation regarding the Báb, His teachings and what really transpired at the incident. However, the fact that this worldwide publicity occurred just nineteen months after the Declaration of the Báb, is an indicator of the divine source of His message.

4. Spreading the Seeds of Faith

After their expulsion from Shíráz, the three brave Bábís visited various cities teaching and propagating the Message of the Báb with zeal and ardor. Their travels included a visit to Ardistán where they enlisted Mírzá Fatḥ 'Alí, who became a distinguished believer. His son later married the daughter of Mullá 'Alí-Akbar. Sometime later the group split up and headed in different directions. Quddús went to Kirmán while Ṣádiq left for the fanatical city of Yazd.

The main interest of Mullá Ṣádiq in going to Yazd was to satisfy his curiosity about the activities of Mírzá Aḥmad who had spent a long period of his life writing a compilation containing 12,000 Islamic traditions concerning the advent of the Qá'im, the Promised Messenger of Shí'ih Islam.

Mullá Ṣádiq went directly to the mosque where Mírzá Aḥmad was giving a sermon. Enthused by his recent experiences in Shíraz Mullá Ṣádiq sat in the front row and joined the congregational prayer. As soon as the ceremony was over, without invitation, he went up to the pulpit and, to the surprise of the faithful, addressed them with one of the famous homilies of the Báb. After which Mullá Ṣádiq intrepidly stated:

> Render thanks to God, O people of learning, for, behold, the Gate of Divine Knowledge, which you deem to have been closed, is now wide open. The River of everlasting life has streamed forth from the city of Shíráz, and is conferring untold blessings upon the people of this land. Whoever has

[160]Moojan Momen. *The Bábí and Bahá'í Religions, 1844-1944: Some Contemporary Western Accounts.* George Ronald Oxford, 1981, p. 69

> partaken of one drop from this Ocean of heavenly grace, no matter how humble and unlettered, has discovered in himself the power to unravel the profoundest mysteries, and has felt capable of expounding the most abstruse themes of ancient wisdom. And whoever, though he be the most learned expounder of the Faith of Islám, has chosen to rely upon his own competence and power and has disdained the Message of God, has condemned himself to irretrievable degradation and loss.[161]

Such words provoked the fanatics. As he addressed the congregation, the crowd began to shout and vilify Mullá Ṣádiq shocked by his revolutionary claims. When he descended from the pulpit they rushed to him and assaulted him, leaving him battered and bruised.

If it had not been for Siyyid Ḥusayn's timely intervention, the damage would have been more serious. Siyyid Ḥusayn, with force and determination, dispersed Mullá Ṣádiq's attackers and stated that he was now in his custody. He insinuated to the crowd that Mullá Ṣádiq was not in his right mind. If he proved sane and if Mullá Ṣádiq's guilt was proven, he promised that crowd that he was committed to applying the corresponding punishment himself.

That was how Mullá Ṣádiq was freed from the danger posed by the crowd. He was then transferred, bruised and without his cane, to Siyyid Ḥusayn's house where he was safe and secure.

It was around the same time when a Letter of the Living named Mullá Yúsuf passed through the city. He also had to suffer from the hands of the local Muslims. Together they decided to leave Yazd for Kirmán. There Mullá Ṣádiq was again exposed to the humiliation and rudeness of Hájí Mírzá Karim Khán, a former disciple of Siyyid Káẓim.

Upon the death of Siyyid Káẓim, Ḥájí Mírzá Karím Khán had declared himself the successor and leader of his movement, disobeying the warnings that Siyyid Káẓim had left. Mullá Ṣádiq had in mind to make him aware for the first time of the Báb's message. For this purpose, he brought with him verses from the Qayyúmu'l-Asmá' which he shared

[161]Nabíl. *The Dawn-Breakers: Nabíl's Narrative of the Early Days of the Bahá'í Revelation.* US Bahá'í Publishing Trust, 1932, p. 186.

with Ḥájí Mírzá Karím Khán.

But all efforts were unsuccessful because Karim Khán was already determined to end the Faith of the Báb and his followers. In his spiritual blindness he had written a treatise attacking the Báb. A.L.M. Nicolas, the French writer and traveler of those times, wrote about what happened at that time:

> A bitter struggle broke out between the Muqaddas and Karím Khán who, as it is known, had taken the rank of chief of the Shaykhí sect, after the death of Kázim. The discussion took place in the presence of many people and Karím challenged his opponent to prove the truth of the mission of the Báb. 'If you succeed,' he said to him, 'I will be converted and my pupils with me; but if you fail, I shall have it proclaimed in the bazaars: "Behold the one who tramples under foot the Holy Law of Islám!"' 'I know who you are, Karím,' replied Muqaddas to him. 'Do you not remember your Master Siyyid Kázim and that which he told you: "... do you not wish that I should die that, after me, may appear the absolute truth?" Witness how today, urged on by your passion for riches and for glory, you lie to yourself!'
>
> Begun in this vein, the discussion was bound to be brief. Instantly, the pupils of Karím drew their knives and threw themselves upon him who was insulting their chief. Fortunately, the governor of the city interposed; Muqaddas was arrested and brought to his house where he kept him for a while and, when the excitement had subsided, he sent him away by night, escorted for several miles by ten mounted men.[162]

5. Among the Companions of Tabarsí

Despite the difficulties encountered in spreading the Faith in those early years, in Shíráz, Yazd and Kirmán, Mullá Ṣádiq had to endure some of his greatest moments in the episode of the Fort Tabarsí, where he was an active participant.

[162]Nabíl. *The Dawn-Breakers: Nabíl's Narrative of the Early Days of the Bahá'í Revelation.* US Bahá'í Publishing Trust, 1932, p. 187.

Following his stay in Kirmán, Mullá Ṣádiq went to his native Khurásán where he was well known and highly esteemed. At his home in Mashhad he held teaching meetings where he taught the Faith of the Báb.

Those were the days when Mullá Ḥusayn built the Bábíyyih (the Bábí House) in the same city of Mashhad. It was erected at the Báb's instructions to become a centre to teach the Faith and attracted believers from all over Persia. "A steady stream of visitors," explains Nabíl in his *Narrative*, "whom the energy and zeal of Mullá Ḥusayn had prepared for the acceptance of the Faith, poured into the presence of Quddús, acknowledged the claim of the Cause, and willingly enlisted under its banner." [163] This uncontrollable avalanche of enthusiasm and fervor, grew day by day, under the fearful watch of the Muslim clergy.

On July 21, 1848, Mullá Ḥusayn along with 202 Bábís, left the city for the province of Mázindarán. His goal was to fulfill the explicit request of the Báb to help Quddús, who was confined to the house of a cleric. On the way, they went through several towns and attracted new recruits to their courageous band.

However, in the village of Barfurúsh they were received with hostility and therefore were forced to take refuge in an old religious sanctuary later known as the Tabarsí Fort. Due to the threat of assault by government troops, they transformed the shrine into a precarious fort using the few means at their disposal.

From that date until May 1849, the Bábís were actively pursued by the army by order of the Sháh and at the instigation of the clergy. The pain and suffering endured by that heroic group of Bábís was great and indescribable. For a long period they were besieged and this was followed by a slaughter of the faithful.

The food supply was cut off. There was continuous shelling by heavy artillery from the surrounding regiments, coupled with uninterrupted cavalry raids made against the fort defenders. However, to the astonishment of the officers, and indeed the entire nation, for an extended period the army was unable to achieve its goal.

---

[163]Nabíl. *The Dawn-Breakers: Nabíl's Narrative of the Early Days of the Bahá'í Revelation*. US Bahá'í Publishing Trust, 1932, p. 267.

Finally, it became clear that those comrades — a handful of elders and students of religion — were imbued with a supernatural power, which was difficult to subjugate by the power of arms.

Among the defenders was Mullá Ṣádiq who despite his advanced age, had an important role in the events. 'Abdu'l-Bahá makes special mention of Mullá Ṣádiq when he points out in the book *Memorials of the Faithful* that for 18 days they faced total starvation. The men were reduced by agonizing hunger to devour the leather of their shoes and the grass that grew in the surroundings. In the morning after taking a mouthful of water they laid on the floor waiting for the next confrontation. However, when attacked they all rose to defend themselves like the great heroes of antiquity.

Such courage was supported by a strong spirituality, firmness of faith and complete trust in God, all attributes that surprised the opposite forces. This state of affairs continued until May 1849 when, through deception, the army was able to take the fort and martyr the Bábís gathered within its precincts.

These believers, victims of a military force that greatly outnumbered them, were killed in the most atrocious way. Nabíl's *Narrative* documents the magnitude of the savagery that the Persian people incurred at that time.

Some of eminent and distinguished position, like Mullá Ṣádiq, were saved from the massacre, because the officers hoped to obtain a ransom in exchange for their liberation. Those few survivors were able to relate the story of those fateful days in detail.

At the end of the siege, Mullá Ṣádiq along with other Bábís, was chained and paraded through the streets of Bárfurúsh accompanied by the sound of drums.

'Abdu'l-Bahá related the fate of Mullá Ṣádiq:

> They took him prisoner at the Fort and delivered him over to the chiefs of Mázindarán, to lead him about and finally kill him in a certain district of that province. When, bound with chains, Mullá Ṣádiq was brought to the appointed place, God put it into one man's heart to free him from prison in the middle of the night and guide him to a place where he was

safe. [164]

On his return from Fort Tabarsi he had to live in hiding but he was firmer than ever in the Cause of God. Eventually he resumed his teaching activities with great fervor. He became a bright torch in the field of service. In spite of constant separation from his family, Mullá Ṣádiq continued to demonstrate complete devotion and consecration.

'Abdu'l-Bahá posthumously named Mullá Ṣádiq a Hand of the Cause of God. With the passage of time, his son Mírzá 'Alí Muḥammad proved to be worthy of his father's spiritual heritage and for the services he rendered and his loyalty to the Faith, Bahá'u'lláh named him among the first four Hands of the Cause of God.

6. In Baghdád

Sometime later, around 1861, Mullá Ṣádiq traveled to the city of Baghdád where he had the honor and blessing of meeting Bahá'u'lláh. By that time, Bahá'u'lláh had not yet made His mission public, and was known as Jináb-i-Bahá (His Highness, the Glory).

Such was the rejoicing of Mullá Ṣádiq when he entered the presence of Bahá'u'lláh that he was instantly transformed. As Bahá'u'lláh had not yet revealed His Mission, the believers were still unaware of His station. Hence they were very surprised to see Mullá Ṣádiq's reverence and complete humility in front of his Beloved. Mullá Ṣádiq was a revered character among the Bábís of Persia. Intoxicated with joy, for fourteen months Mullá Ṣádiq forgot the world around him, after which he was instructed to return to his native Khurásán. A believer related the details of such visit:

> One afternoon I was seated in the room talking with Mullá Muḥammad-Sádiq-i-Khurásání, known as Muqaddas.[4] He was a learned man of great dignity and stature. As we were talking together, Bahá'u'lláh, Who had just returned from the town, arrived in the outer apartment accompanied by Prince Mulk-Ára whose hand He was holding. Mullá Sádiq, who was the embodiment of dignity and solemnity, immediately rose

[164] 'Abdu'l-Bahá. *Memorials of the Faithful.* Wilmette, Bahá'í Publishing Trust, 1971, p. 7.

> to his feet and prostrated himself at the feet of Bahá'u'lláh. This action did not please Bahá'u'lláh Who angrily rebuked Mullá Sádiq and ordered him to rise immediately, after which He went out of the room followed by the Prince.
>
> I was amazed and bewildered at such behaviour on the part of Mullá Sádiq as I had never expected such an important person to act in this manner. Having witnessed Bahá'u'lláh's reaction also, I expressed my disapproval of Mullá Sádiq's behaviour and admonished him for it, saying: 'You are a man who occupies an exalted position in the realm of knowledge and learning and, above all else, you had the honour of attaining the presence of the Báb Himself. Your rank is next to the Letters of the Living and you are one of the Witnesses of the Dispensation of the Báb. It is true that Bahá'u'lláh is an eminent person Who belongs to the nobility and His ancestors have occupied high positions in the government. It is also true that He has suffered persecution and imprisonment as a result of embracing the Cause of God, that all His possessions have been confiscated and that He has finally been exiled to this land. Yet, your behaviour towards Him this afternoon was like that of an unworthy servant towards his glorious Lord.'
>
> Mullá Sádiq refrained from answering me. He was in a state of spiritual intoxication, his face beaming with joy; he merely said to me, 'I beseech God to tear asunder the veil for thee and shower His bounties upon thy person through His abundant grace.'[165]

Mullá Ṣádiq had a very jovial way of teaching the Faith. 'Abdu'l-Bahá narrates an incident from the days of Ba<u>gh</u>dád:

> After he had come to Ba<u>gh</u>dád and attained the presence of Bahá'u'lláh, he was seated one day in the courtyard of the men's apartments, by the little garden. I was in one of the rooms just above, that gave onto the courtyard. At that moment a Persian prince, a grandson of Fath-'Alí <u>Sh</u>áh,

[165]Adib Taherzadeh. *The Revelation of Bahá'u'lláh,* vol 1. George Ronald Oxford, 1974, pp. 92-93.

> arrived at the house. The prince said to him, "Who are you?" Mullá Ṣádiq answered, "I am a servant of this Threshhold. I am one of the keepers of this door." And as I listened from above, he began to teach the Faith. The prince at first objected violently; and yet, in a quarter of an hour, gently and benignly, Jináb-i-Mullá Ṣádiq had quieted him down. After the prince had so sharply denied what was said, and his face had so clearly reflected his fury, now his wrath was changed to smiles and he expressed the greatest satisfaction at having encountered Mullá Ṣádiq and heard what he had to say.[166]

According to 'Abdu'l-Bahá, "He always taught cheerfully and with gaiety, and would respond gently and with good humor, no matter how much passionate anger might be turned against him by the one with whom he spoke. His way of teaching was excellent. He was truly Mullá Ṣádiq, the Name of God, not for his fame but because he was a chosen soul."[167]

7. In the Síyáh Chal

During 1860-1862 a campaign of persecution against the believers in Tehran was unleashed and Mullá Ṣádiq fell victim to it along with his young son.[168] This time, he was arrested with his young son and imprisoned for twenty-eight months in the Síyáh Chal also called "Black Hole". This was an underground dungeon infested with filth and vermin. It had previously been one of the water tanks of a public bath in the city. Years before, in 1853, Bahá'u'lláh was imprisoned in the same prison, and it was there that He received the first intimations of His divine mission.

---

[166]'Abdu'l-Bahá. *Memorials of the Faithful.* Wilmette, Bahá'í Publishing Trust, 1971, p. 6.

[167]'Abdu'l-Bahá. *Memorials of the Faithful.* Wilmette, Bahá'í Publishing Trust, 1971, p. 6.

[168]Interestingly, Mullá Ṣádiq's son became known as Ibn-i-Aṣdaq (the son of Aṣdaq) and was appointed a Hand of the Cause by Bahá'u'lláh. Ibn-i-Aṣdaq asked for martyrdom in His path but instead he lived a long life (1850-1928) teaching the Bahá'í Faith. Bahá'u'lláh addressed him as "Sháhíd ibn-i-Sháhíd" (Martyr, son of the Martyr).

One day, the child Ibn-i-Aṣdaq fell ill in the prison and it was necessary for a doctor to come. A Jewish doctor from the royal court came who managed to heal the boy. The doctor was very impressed by the knowledge and personality of Mullá Ṣádiq that he kept returning to the dungeon to talk with him for long hours. In the end, the doctor was led by Mullá Ṣádiq to recognize the Truth. His name was Hakim Masih and he is known as the first believer of Jewish origin in Persia. Shortly after that conversion a large number of people of that religion accepted the Faith, especially in the Hamadan region, where one day Mullá Ṣádiq would rest forever.

According to Hasan Balyuzi:

> Many well-known men who were acquainted with him visited him in Siyah-Chal and tried hard to induce him to write a few lines which they could show to Násirí'd-Dín Sháh and obtain his release. But he consistently refused to comply with their wishes and make any appeal. He wrote: 'It is shameful that a man in need should appeal to another one in need.' Thus he stayed for twenty-eight months in that prison. Then Násirí'd-Dín Sháh, of his own accord, ordered his release. Mullá Ṣádiq refused to leave the dungeon without his fellow-prisoners. He had pledged his word to them, he said, that they would leave Siyah-Chal together. When the Sháh learned of Mullá Ṣádiq's stand he was amazed, but asked for a list of all the inmates of Siyah-Chal. Besides Mullá Ṣádiq, there were forty-three names in that list. All but three were pardoned, and those three had been arrested only recently and were guilty men. [169]

In subsequent years, Mullá Ṣádiq taught the Faith to high status individuals in Iranian society. Hasan Balyuzi related how he, in the years subsequent to his release from prison, was a guest of 'Aynu'l-Mulk, the brother of the Sháh's mother. He also interacted with other members of the Tiḥrán aristocracy:

On two occasions Mullá Ṣádiq was taken to the Inspectorate which was in the charge of 'Aynu'l-Mulk. There he said: "Some of these men

[169]Hasan Balyuzi. *Eminent Bahá'ís in the Time of Bahá'u'lláh.* George Ronald Oxford, 1985, pp. 18-19.

have been in this prison for seven years. They have no clothing left, are bare and in utter misery. They ought to be clad and allowed to go home in peace. The authorities should provide them with suitable clothes and money and send them home, bring some joy into their miserable lives." His praiseworthy initiative led to the introduction of the Faith of God in all the areas where these people lived. Its abiding results will endure forever. The descendants and the clans of those men remain within the fold of the Faith, ever ready to be of service to others.

> After departing from the house of 'Aynu'l-Mulk, Mullá Ṣádiq stayed for three days in the mosque of Sipahsalar. From there he moved to the house of Muḥammad-Vali Mírzá (a son of Fath-'Alí Sháh), who was greatly attached to him. His sojourn there lasted nineteen days, and there he came face to face with a number of very influential divines of Ṭihrán, such as Hájí Mullá 'Alíy-i-Kani and Siyyid Ṣádiq-i-Sanglaji. These men had heard of the vast learning of Mullá Ṣádiq. One after the other, in rapid succession, they asked him intricate questions and posed him many problems to resolve. It must be said that none of those divines was favourably inclined towards the Faith of Bahá'u'lláh. Indeed, the two already named were bitterly hostile. Hájí Mullá 'Alíy-i-Kaní was the man who, when given Bahá'u'lláh's Tablet to Násirí'd-Dín Sháh so that he might write an answer to it, treated the matter with great disdain. Now, they all fell under the spell of the speech of Mullá Ṣádiq. None of them, however hard he tried, could match, let alone surpass his deep knowledge, his eloquence, his logic and measured speech.
>
> When these proceedings in the home of his relative were reported to Násirí'd-Dín Sháh, he, of all the people, upbraided Hisamu's-Saltanih (his own uncle) for condemning such a man as Mullá Ṣádiq to imprisonment. He ordered two of his best horses, richly saddled, to be given to Mullá Ṣádiq, as well as a gift of money. The mother of Násirí'd-Dín Sháh, who was present that day in the house of Muḥammad-Valí Mírzá and sitting with a number of other ladies of high rank behind a curtain, was listening to the trial of strength between

> Mullá Ṣádiq and the divines of Ṭihrán; she presented him with rich, valuable clothes befitting his rank. Mullá Ṣádiq courteously returned all the royal gifts and wrote a letter to the Sháh expressing his gratitude. Then he borrowed a sum of money from a fellow-believer in Ṭihrán and took the road to Khurásán. It was then that he helped Hájí Mírzá Muḥammad-Ridá, the Mu'taminu's-Saltanih, the future Vazir of Khurásán, to embrace the Faith of Bahá'u'lláh.
>
> Three years later, Mullá Ṣádiq returned to Ṭihrán and helped in changing the secret hiding-place of the remains of the Báb. Having performed that service, urgently required, he left the capital once again and visited Ká<u>sh</u>án, Iṣfahán and Yazd. Everywhere he went he fearlessly and energetically taught and propagated the Faith of Bahá'u'lláh. But his most outstanding service was that which he rendered in Yazd. There, some of the Afnans (relatives of the Báb) were still hesitant and uncommitted; Mullá Ṣádiq made them see and totally accept the truth of the new Theophany. After this remarkable achievement, he returned to his native province of Khurásán where, for six years, he travelled throughout that province teaching, continuously teaching. During that time he was constantly attacked, reviled and denounced by adversaries. [170]

When Mullá Ṣádiq's son grew up he was called Ibn-i-Aṣdaq (the son of Aṣdaq) and was later appointed a Hand of the Cause of God by Bahá'u'lláh. Once Ibn-i-Aṣdaq asked Bahá'u'lláh for martyrdom in His path but instead he lived a long live (1850-1928) teaching the Bahá'í Faith. Bahá'u'lláh addressed him as Sháhíd Ibn-i-Sháhíd (Martyr, son of the Martyr).

8. Pilgrimage to 'Akká

From Ba<u>gh</u>dád, Bahá'u'lláh was exiled to the city of Adrianople. It was in this period that Mullá Ṣádiq heard about the exalted position of Bahá'u'lláh as the greatest Manifestation of God. Aware as he was of

[170]Hasan Balyuzi. *Eminent Bahá'ís in the Time of Bahá'u'lláh*. George Ronald Oxford, 1985, pp. 20-21.

that reality, he joyfully embraced the Faith of Bahá'u'lláh.

Some years later, while residing in the Most Great Prison, Bahá'u'lláh revealed a Tablet in his honor inviting Mullá Ṣádiq to attain His presence. Mullá Ṣádiq was very old and was at that time residing in Khurásán. In that Tablet he is instructed to travel in the company of another Bahá'í because of his age and the journey, leaving his child at home.

Mullá Ṣádiq arrived in 'Akká, probably at the beginning of the year 1874. He stayed several months in 'Akká surrounded by that heavenly atmosphere until the time when Bahá'u'lláh, in a Tablet, advised him to return home. Hasan Balyuzi wrote about this pilgrimage:

> Ill and exhausted, his dearest wish now was to attain, once again, the presence of Bahá'u'lláh. Before long that wish was realized. Bahá'u'lláh summoned him to 'Akká. When that call reached him he was revived. He sent word that he desired the people to come and visit him. They came, and to them, Bahá'í or non-Bahá'í alike, he gave such advice as would serve them well in days to come. His visitors were greatly moved. His words came from a heart pure and unsullied, from a soul brave and constant, leaving a deep impression on all who were privileged to hear him, and evoking a response commensurate with his earnestness. A good many wished to accompany and serve him in his pilgrimage. Bahá'u'lláh had, however, directed him to bring only one person with him, and those who wished to be with him vied for that honour. Mírzá Ja'far was the man who secured it. His son, the future Hand of the Cause Ibn-i-Aṣdaq accompanied them until they reached Sabzivar. There he offered his father a small sum of money which he did not accept.
>
> The route which Mullá Ṣádiq took was through Caucasia [the western Russian – Istanbul route]. It was a long and tiring journey, but he stood up to its hardships. And, at long last, he found himself in the presence of Bahá'u'lláh. He had lived expectantly for that moment. All his toils, his sufferings, spread over so many years were forgotten at that supreme moment, and for four months he had the bounty of living close to his Lord. At the end of that period of untold bliss the

Tongue of Grandeur thus addressed him:

> "O My name, the Aṣdaq! Render thanks unto God that We called thee to appear before the Seat of Glory, to hear Us and to witness the Light of the Countenance of thy Lord, the Exalted, the Mighty, the Single, the Supreme; and We sent thee back to inform the people of what thou hast seen and understood, and to call them to the utmost constancy, lest their steps falter at the clamour of any corrupt pretender. O My name! recall every day Our counsel to thee in Our Presence. Verily, thy Lord is the All-Knowing, the All-Informed." [171]

In several Tablets, the Blessed Beauty revealed the holy and heroic position of Mullá Ṣádiq. Among them are Lawḥ-i-Ahbáb (Tablet of Friends) and the Lawḥ-i-Mubáhilih (Tablet of the Confrontation). It is estimated that Bahá'u'lláh and 'Abdu'l-Bahá addressed approximately 250 Tablets to Mullá Ṣádiq and his descendants.[172] The Lawḥ-i-Ahbáb has not yet been translated, however, Adib Taherzadeh has summarized it in the following terms:

> Bahá'u'lláh exhorts the believers to steadfastness in His Cause and to detachment from everything beside God, and to unity among themselves. He reminds them that He has accepted sufferings and tribulations so that mankind might become united. He warns them never, therefore, to allow differences to enter their midst. He gives them a commandment: first to live their lives in accordance with His teachings and then to conquer the hearts of men in His Name by holy deeds and exalted character. He enjoins on them to teach the Cause with wisdom, counsels them to arise for the triumph of His Faith in such wise that no earthly power can deter them from executing their purpose, assures them that the glances of His loving-kindness are directed towards

---

[171] Hasan Balyuzi. *Eminent* Bahá'í*s in the Time of* Bahá'u'lláh. *George* Ronald Oxford, 1985, p.22.

[172] Vahid Rafati. ḴORĀSĀNI, MOLLĀ ṢĀDEQ. Ency*clopædia Iranica,* online edition, 2016, available at http://www.iranicaonline.org/articles/khorasani-molla-sadeq (accessed on 29 June 2019).

> them, and prophesies the advent of a day when the banners of victory will be planted in every city, when the peoples of the world will glory in the believers' names and lament over all the sufferings they have borne in the path of their Lord.[173]

The Tablet of Mubalílih was revealed in Adrianople when Bahá'u'lláh publicly confronted Mírzá Yahyá about his claims to divine revelation and about his antagonism. Only the following passage has been translated by Shoghi Effendi:

> O Muḥammad! He Who is the Spirit hath, verily, issued from His habitation, and with Him have come forth the souls of God's chosen ones and the realities of His Messengers. Behold, then, the dwellers of the realms on high above Mine head, and all the testimonies of the Prophets in My grasp. Say: Were all the divines, all the wise men, all the kings and rulers on earth to gather together, I, in very truth, would confront them, and would proclaim the verses of God, the Sovereign, the Almighty, the All-Wise. I am He Who feareth no one, though all who are in heaven and all who are on earth rise up against me.... This is Mine hand which God hath turned white for all the worlds to behold. This is My staff; were We to cast it down, it would, of a truth, swallow up all created things.[174]

Many beautiful testimonies from the pen of 'Abdu'l-Bahá testify to Mullá Ṣádiq's station and services:

> He was like a surging sea, a falcon that soared high. His visage shone, his tongue was eloquent, his strength and steadfastness astounding. When he opened his lips to teach, the proofs would stream out; when he chanted or prayed, his eyes shed tears like a spring cloud. His face was luminous, his life spiritual, his knowledge both acquired and innate; and celestial was his ardor, his detachment from the world,

---

[173]Adib Taherzadeh. *The Revelation of Bahá'u'lláh*, vol 4. George Ronald Oxford, 1974, p. 259.

[174]Adapted from: Shoghi Effendi. *God Passes By.* US Bahá'í Publishing Trust, 1979, pp. 168-169.

his righteousness, his piety and fear of God.[175]

The circumstances of his death following his pilgrimage were also extraordinary:

> The time had come for parting from the presence of Bahá'u'lláh and he turned homewards by way of Mosul and Baghdád. All along that route he gave the people he met the tidings of the advent of the Day of God. Physically he was exhausted, but his spirit shone as bright as ever. His dedicated soul knew no repose except in obeying the command of his Lord. When he reached Hamadan, his physical strength had touched its nadir, but not the bravery of his soul. He stayed for twelve days in Hamadan, never resting. On the last day he told his servitors to bring him his best, his most costly clothes. He put them on, using a good deal of rose-water and perfume. Then he asked those who were with him to leave him alone for an hour. At the end of that hour he called them back, and asked one of them to help him undress. He had only one arm out of his sleeve when he said to the man who was helping him, 'That is enough'; the next moment he was gone--gone from this world. Thus, calmly and serenely, death brought release to Mullá Sádiq, Ismu'lláhu'l-Aṣdaq, from untold tribulations which would have broken a lesser man, but were endured by him with radiant acquiescence in the path of his Lord. His death occurred in the year 1889. [176]
>
> Ismu'lláh's tomb is in Hamadán. Many a Tablet was revealed for him by the Supreme Pen of Bahá'u'lláh, including a special Visitation Tablet after his passing. He was a great personage, perfect in all things.
>
> Such blessed beings have now left this world. Thank God, they did not linger on, to witness the agonies that followed the Ascension of Bahá'u'lláh—the intense afflictions; for firmly rooted mountains will shake and tremble at these,

[175]'Abdu'l-Bahá. *Memorials of the Faithful.* Wilmette, Bahá'í Publishing Trust, 1971, p. 8.

[176]Hasan Balyuzi. *Eminent Bahá'íS in the Time of Bahá'u'lláh.* George Ronald Oxford, 1985, pp.22-23.

and the high-towering hills bow down.

He was truly Mullá Ṣádiq, the Name of God. Fortunate is the one who circumambulates that tomb, who blesses himself with the dust of that grave. Upon him be salutations and praise in the Abhá Realm.[177]

[177]'Abdu'l-Bahá. *Memorials of the Faithful.* Wilmette, Bahá'í Publishing Trust, 1971, p. 8.

Bibliography

'Abdu'l-Bahá. *A Traveler's Narrative.* US Bahá'í Publishing Trust, 1980.

'Abdu'l-Bahá. *Paris Talks.* UK Bahá'í Publishing Trust, 1972.

Afroukhteh, Youness. *Memories of Nine Years in 'Akká* (translated by Riaz Masrour). George Ronald Oxford, 2004.

Ayman, Iraj. *Principles of Bahá'í Theology in the Tablet of Salmán.* Paper presented at the Irfan Colloquia. Louhelen Bahá'í School, Michigan, October 9-12, 1988.

Bahá'í World Centre. Bahá'í Calendar, Festivals, and Dates of Historic Significance. The Bahá'í World (1979-1983), Vol. 18 Haifa, 1986.

Bahá'u'lláh. *Gleanings from the Writings of Bahá'u'lláh.* US Bahá'í Publishing Trust, 1990.

Bahá'u'lláh. *The Kitáb-i-Íqán.* US Bahá'í Publishing Trust, 1989.

Balyuzi, Hasan. *Bahá'u'lláh, the King of Glory.* George Ronald Oxford, 1991.

Balyuzi, Hasan. *Eminent Bahá'ís in the Time of Bahá'u'lláh.* George Ronald Oxford, 1985.

Brookshaw, Dominic Parviz. Letters to Bahá'í princesses: Tablets revealed in honour of the women of Ibn-i Aṣdaq's household. Lights of Irfan, volume 5, 2003, pp. 17-40. Available on line at: http://irfancolloquia.org/pdf/lights5_brookshaw.pdf

Browne, Edward Granville. *Materials for the Study of the Bábí Religion.* Cambridge, 1918.

Browne, Edward Granville. The Bábís of Persia II – Their Literature and Doctrines. *The Journal of the Royal Asiatic Society of Great Britain and Ireland,* vol. 4, No. 4, 1889.

Gail, Marzieh. *Dawn Over Mount Hira and Other Essays.* George Ronald Oxford, 1976. Available online at: https://bahai-library.com/pdf/g/gail_dawn_mount_hira.pdf

Haji Mírzá Haydar 'Alí. *Stories from the Delight of Hearts - Memoirs of Haji Mírzá Haydar-* 'Alí. (translated by Abu'l-Qasim Faizi). Kalimat Press, 1995.

Hatcher, John S. and Hemmat, Amrollah. *Reunion with the Beloved: Poetry and Martyrdom.* Juxta Publishing Limited, Hong Kong, 2014, p. 82-83. Available online at: https://bahai-library.com/pdf/h/hatcher_hemmat_poetry_martyrdom.pdf

Lewis, Frank. Poetry as Revelation: Introduction to Bahá'u'lláh's 'Mathnavíy-i Mubárak'. *Bahá'í Studies Review,* 9. London: Association for Bahá'í Studies English-Speaking Europe, 1999. Available on: https://bahai-library.com/lewis_poetry_revelation

Mehrabkhani, R. *El Esplendor del Dia Prometido.* Editorial Bahá'í de España, 1974.

Mírzá Habíbu'lláh Afnán. *Memories of the Báb, Bahá'u'lláh and `Abdu'l-Bahá* (Translated and Annotated by Ahang Rabbani). An electronic-publication of Kalimat Press, 2005.

Momen, Moojan. *Bahá'u'lláh: A Short Biography.* London, Oneworld Publications, 2007.

Momen, Moojan. *The Bábí and Bahá'í Religions, 1844-1944: Some Contemporary Western Accounts.* George Ronald Oxford, 1981.

Momen, Moojan. *The Bahá'í Communities of Iran.* George Ronald Oxford, 2015.

Momen, Moojan. Memorials of the Faithful: The Democratization of Sainthood. *Lights of Irfan,* vol. 17, 2015, pp. 205-224. Available online at: http://irfancolloquia.org/pdf/lights17_momen_sainthood.pdf

Munirih Khánum. *Episodes in the Life of Munírih Khánum* (translated by Mirza Ahmad Sohrab.) Los Angeles: Persian American Publishing Company, 1924.

Nabíl Zarandí. *Mathnaví-i-Nabíl-i-Zarandí.* Langenhain, Germany: Bahá'í Verlag, 1995.

Nabíl-e Zarandi. *Masnavi-ye Nabíl-e Zarandi dar târikh-e amr-e Bahâ'i va so'ud-e Hazrat-e Bahâ Allâh.* Cairo: Mohyi al-Din Sabri-ye Kordi, 1924.

Rafati, Vahid. NABIL-E AʿẒAM ZARANDI, MOLLĀ MOḤAMMAD. *Encyclopædia Iranica*, online edition, 2016, available at http://www.iranicaonline.org/articles/nabil-zarandi (accessed on 29 June 2019).

Rafati, Vahid ḴORĀSĀNI, MOLLĀ ṢĀDEQ. Encyclopædia Iranica, online edition, 2016, available at http://www.iranicaonline.org/articles/khorasani-molla-sadeq (accessed on 29 June 2019).

Ruhe, David S. *Door of Hope: A Century of the Bahá'í Faith in the Holy Land.* George Ronald Oxford, 1983.

Shoghi Effendi. *The Advent of Divine Justice.* US Bahá'í Publishing Trust, 1990.

Shoghi Effendi. *The Promised Day Is Come.* US Bahá'í Publishing Trust, 1980.

Taherzadeh, Adib. The Revelation of Bahá'u'lláh. Oxford, U. K.: George Ronald, 1977.

Zarqani Mahmud. *Mahmud's Diary: The Diary of Mirza Mahmud-I-Zarqani: Chronicling 'Abdu'l Baha's Journey to America* (translated by Mohi Sobhani). George Ronald Oxford, 1998.

www.ingramcontent.com/pod-product-compliance
Lightning Source LLC
Chambersburg PA
CBHW020325010526
44107CB00054B/1985
9780648901433